Tempus ORAL HISTORY *Series*

Cardiff
voices

Compiled by
Brian Lee

'We who occupy the scene today walk not in untrodden paths
but in the well-worn steps of our ancestors.'

Cardiff – A History of the City, William Rees, 1962

TEMPUS

First published 2000
Copyright © Brian Lee, 2000

Tempus Publishing Limited
The Mill, Brimscombe Port,
Stroud, Gloucestershire, GL5 2QG

ISBN 0 7524 1653 7

Typesetting and origination by
Tempus Publishing Limited
Printed in Great Britain by
Midway Clark Printing, Wiltshire

This book is dedicated to Bill 'My Cardiff' Barrett of the *Cardiff Post*

The popular Pine Trees Café, Roath Park, c. 1936.

Contents

Duke Street in 1922.

Introduction

This book contains the memories of those Cardiffians who grew up in the town before 1955, when it became the capital city of Wales. It tells the stories of inhabitants who lived through the 1920s and '30s as well as those, like myself, who grew up in the Cardiff of the 1940s and '50s. In the following pages you will meet people who lived, worked and played in a community which, over the years, has seen many changes.

A few of the interviewees were my own family and friends, but the majority of them were complete strangers before I interviewed them. A number of the memories have been transcribed from tape recordings which are now ten years old: when I was co-ordinator of the, sadly now defunct, City Hall-based Historic Records Project, I decided that I would send a team of researchers armed with tape recorders to interview some of the older citizens of Cardiff and have them tell of their life's experiences. I had copies made of those tapes in the hope that one day they would prove useful. That day has now arrived and it is good to think that, although some of those interviewees will no longer be with us – they were in their eighties when interviewed – their memories have been recorded for posterity.

The only previous collection of general reminiscences of Cardiffians, as far as I know, was compiled in Volume V of John Hobson Matthews' *Records of the County Borough of Cardiff* published between 1898 and 1905. In this volume, a Mr William Luke Evans, then aged eighty-four, recalled: 'I remember the last ale-taster of Cardiff. His name was Edward Philpot and his nickname Toby Philpot. I well remember hearing him say to someone with whom he was talking in the street: "Well, I must go now and see what sort of ale they have got at the Glove

Queen Street, c. 1920.

and Shears." One day coming out of church, we saw a hare bolt out of the Blue Bell. We chased it into the Cardiff Arms yard where it was caught. We had it for dinner a few days afterwards.' The Glove and Shears Inn, which dated back to 1792, was situated at 26 Duke Street and like Mr William Luke Evans is now long gone. As for the Blue Bell Inn, in High Street, it is still there, but sadly is now known as The Goat Major.

Another old inhabitant could remember a man being tied to a cart's tail, for some heinous offence, and dragged and flogged through the market held in High Street where they used to put wrongdoers in the stocks.

Yet another could recall seeing the body of Richard Lewis (Dick Penderyn) who was hanged for participating in the Merthyr Riots of 1831. On a pleasanter note, one interviewee recollected: 'The tidal harbour of Cardiff was situated where Westgate Street now stands. Quay Street was the entrance to the shipping, where passengers were taken on board the market-boats bound for Bristol. If these had started, the last place for shipment was the Golate, the lane between the Queen's Hotel and the South Wales News offices. Hence its present name'. The Golate lane still exists, of course, but the newspaper offices of the *South Wales News*, later to become the *South Wales Echo*, have now become an office block known as Golate House. The Queen's Hotel is now, or was the last time I looked, the Bank of Ireland.

How times change. Cardiff has always had its fair share of eccentric characters and some of those as recalled in the old borough records are: 'Peg the Wash', an old washerwoman who used to chase children with a stick; 'Hairy Mick', a lamplighter whose beard ran down to his ankles;

Advertisement boards on Newport Road in the 1930s.

'Cough Candy', a dwarfish vendor of cough sweets, whose tall hat was covered in advertisements; and 'Stibbs the Barber' who was always playing jokes on people. In my day it was 'Larbo the Tramp', 'Blocko', who sold tram blocks from a hand cart, and more recently a poor soul who walked the streets with a lavatory seat around his neck which he wore like a mayor's chain of office.

It is also recorded that when the town council in 1886 changed the name Crockherbtown to Queen Street there were many objections. Alas, all to no avail. A Cardiff Directory for 1858 informs us that on the approach to the villas in Crockherbtown there were to be found neatly kept flower beds while dwarf shrubs and evergreens gave graceful taste to the increasing number of respectable inhabitants. One of these inhabitants had this to say about his house: 'It had a beautiful old fashioned and wonderfully productive garden. I grew figs and mulberries there, and there was mistletoe growing on the apple trees. In those days the theatre stood where the Park Hall stands now, and there was a lane known as Bradley's Lane going up where Park Place is now. Mr Bradley's father was a hunting man and had large stables in Womanby Street.'

Just like these reminiscences, and the ones in the old borough records, the memories in *Cardiff Voices* are sometimes sad, sometimes funny and sometimes poetic. And now the time has come to hand you over to all those kindly people who gave of their time to share their memories with us.

Brian Lee

CHAPTER 1
Family and Home

The Jenkins family, c. 1936.

59 Frederick Street

I was born in 59 Frederick Street, in 1926, and was the last of the eight children my mother had. The boys were Walter, Jimmy, Billy, John and me and the girls were Joanna, Eileen and Elsie. 1926 was a bad year to be born because of the General Strike. We were brought up fairly well off. My father was a coal trimmer in the 1930s and we seemed to be a little better off than most people in the area. There was always plenty of food on the table. Frederick Street was a row of terraced houses and it was a long street which went right up to Queen Street with warehouses and a chapel half way up. The Glamorgan Canal was around the back in Hills Terrace and as kids we would swim in the canal in the

Billy, John and Philip Donovan, c. 1929.

summer. It wasn't very clean. Sometimes there would be dead dogs floating in it and of course the water rats. But as boys we didn't mind, as we didn't have the money to go to Guildford Baths.

Philip Donovan

Women stayed Home

In my days the women stayed home and looked after the family. It's different today, they all go to work. The Second World War started that.

Gladys Jenkins

Very Strict

My father was very strict. He wouldn't allow me to drink, smoke or go dancing. And when I went to work in Bath during the war, I abided by his wishes.

Emily Donovan

Airship over Grangetown

I was born in December 1915 and some of my earliest recollections are of incidents at the end of the Great War which impressed themselves on the memory of a two- to three-year-old child. I can remember all the factory hooters sounding off at 11 a.m. on Armistice Day 1918. I remember squads of men marching in fours from Virgil Street school, then a military hospital, up Penarth Road towards the General Station. I can remember an airship flying over Grangetown in the dark with its searchlight shining down to the ground below.

Incidentally, I was cycling to work along the Taff Embankment one Sunday morning in 1931 when the Graf Zeppelin cruised over the south of Cardiff on a brief flight, one of its few over Britain.

Stanley J. Adams

Ada Llewellyn

I remember a lady living in the street named Ada Llewellyn and she belonged to the Dalton Street Methodist church. I remember seeing the old-fashioned fire range in her house: the old kettles and the brass. She still kept things as they were. I can remember she told me that her father was a military man and that she was brought up in Maindy Barracks. She used to be an agent for Singers sewing machines and was very well known all over Cathays.

My mother went to Dalton Street Methodist Sisterhood. She became president of the Sisterhood Guild. They would have different speakers, concerts, tea and cakes, musical afternoons and choirs. It was her life.

Tegwen Hugglestone

Including a Dustbin

My mother, Vera Braddick, married my father Len Bray at Bradford-on-Tone, Somerset, in September 1930 and came to live in Cardiff where my father worked in

Mrs Ada Llewellyn.

11

Members of Dalton Street Methodist church, c. 1950.

Cross Brothers, the large ironmongery business then in St Mary Street and Working Street. They purchased a new house built by George Coffin at No. 5 Gelligaer Gardens, Cathays, for £575, including a dustbin!

Geoff Bray

Benjamin Bird

My grandfather, Benjamin Bird, and his brother Jack kept a shoe repair business at Broadway. Benjamin met his future wife, Hilda Dane, who lived opposite in her father's bakery. The Dane family had

previously had a baker's shop in Dalton Street. Once married, Benjamin and Hilda spent over sixty years living in Tewkesbury Street, Cathays. Their daughter, Doreen, my mother, was one of a few in her class in Gladstone School to survive a severe diphtheria outbreak in 1930.

Sheila Long

Community Spirit

After the war they knocked all the houses down in town and moved the people out. And although we were a good community and everyone knew one another, what did

Bird's Boot Repairing Shop, Broadway, c. 1910.

the council do? They split everybody up to different parts of Cardiff, so that all the good community spirit we had before the war was gone. Now they build community centres to get people together.

Philip Donovan

Domestic Duties

Before the 1939-45 war, domestic duties followed a set daily routine. The water in the copper boiler in the scullery was heated by the coal fire early on Monday morning, when clothes were washed on a washing board. This was followed by scrubbing the tiles in the passage the kitchen and the scullery.

The other downstairs rooms and bedrooms were cleaned on the following

Midland Bank (now HBSC), on Broadway.

weekdays, with Saturday free from housework. In those days, spring cleaning religiously took place in the spring. A few days before Christmas the home-made cakes and puddings were taken to the local bakehouses for the actual cooking. The nearest bakehouse to us was in Albert Street lane.

During my youth, milk and bread were delivered to the door by horse and cart. Also salt and firewood by handcart. Tradesmen who were particularly welcome were those calling out 'Hot Cross Buns' on a Good Friday morning. And we would keep a lookout for the cart from which fresh cockles were sold.

Ruth Hobbs

Church Attendance

We attended church each week. For a while I went to the tin church next to Gladstone School, but I wanted to go to Sunday school at Heath Presbyterian church with John Burgess, and the whole family transferred with me. One Sunday both families were walking to church when an adult commented on the length of the prayers. The minister always mentioned every member of the church who was in the forces by name during prayers. As it happened, I had been given a watch for my birthday, and at the end of the prayer I said in a stage whisper, to the embarrassment of my parents: Seven minutes, thirty seconds.

The church formed a major part of my teenage life because of the Boys' Brigade which I joined in 1945. The festivals of Christmas, Easter, Whitsun and Harvest were enthusiastically celebrated. The Whitsun Treat was usually held at Heath Park, not far away and larger than it is now, and there was great excitement *en route*, with children

Members of Cardiff Comrades Club, Frederick Street, c. 1936.

marching behind the Boys' Brigade band and a special thrill sometimes being allowed to ride on the back of a lorry.

Older church members went early to the field to put up the tents and prepare food and races, and it was interesting to see people who in church seemed quite staid letting their metaphoric hair down. This is a neighbourhood social event which has now gone forever in view of changing social attitudes and supposedly more sophisticated tastes.

My sister Margaret had a sweet clear voice and usually sang a solo, but at one service she read the lesson with great confidence. Closing the large bible with the words 'Here endeth the reading', she completed the performance by taking a flying jump down from the pulpit, much to the surprise of the congregation.

At one Harvest Festival near the end of the war a returning soldier brought a banana which was included in the display. We children gathered around to see this fruit of which we had heard, but which none of us could remember. Nowadays we eat these almost daily.

Geoff Bray

Anna May Wong

I remember Anna May Wong, the American film star, visiting Tiger Bay, but returning [to America] disappointed

15

because there was no Chinatown there any longer. The Tiger Bay area of Butetown used to have a notorious reputation known in seaports all over the world. This may have been justified at one time, but my recollections are of a run-down area of poor underprivileged people many of whom were foreigners, just trying to live.

What I saw, as a telegraph boy, were shabby cafés and many boarding houses where existed swarms of Somali, Lascar and West African seamen, subsisting on curry, fresh air and not much else. There had been a Chinatown once but those canny citizens had departed many years earlier.

Stanley J. Adams

Corner Shops

There were corner shops at most street corners and it was common practice for most housewives to pop over to so and so's for an ounce of this or a bottle of that in order to have a chat with either the shopkeeper or whoever else was in the shop at the time and so break the monotony of being in the house alone.

Jos Dwyer

The Ranch

Anyone who lived in Mynachdy in the 1930s and '40s will know Annie Philips.

Whitsun Treat at Heath Park, c. 1955.

She had a cottage on the canal bank between Maindy and Mynachdy. It was a place where we kids would meet outside of school hours. Two woodbines for a penny or pop and sweets. Sweets were on ration during the war but she would accept next month's coupons. On a Sunday, after playing soccer for about six hours, we would all go to Annie's for our refreshments. Most of us lads called Mynachdy 'The Ranch'. We were all very friendly with the Maindy lads and we would spend our summers swimming in the canal or playing soccer. It cost two pence to go to Llandaff Baths and we never had that to spare.

I was born at 209 Mynachdy Road, in 1928, one of six boys and five girls. I believe they started building the estate about 1920. Number 211 was the last house in the road then and there was a railway bridge. The other side of the bridge was a cottage. The people who lived there, Mr and Mrs John, had no electric or running water. They used a big water butt for the washing water and would get the drinking water from our houses in big cans.

There were no houses on the now Gabalfa estate, nothing but fields and woods and just on the east side of the Taff bridge was an army station with around twenty to thirty soldiers and a big anti-aircraft gun that was our protection against the bombers. Mynachdy Road was the terminus for the buses. The Western Avenue wasn't finished until the late 1930s, and it was indeed a rare sight to see a car travelling along it.

Our village policeman was Bobby Payne who lived at the top of Appledore Road. He wasn't a bully but we avoided him as much as possible. His two sons Harry and Aubrey played soccer with us.

Before the First World War, Peagrams had several shops in Cardiff.

The Regal Dance Hall had fourteen snooker tables and was where the flyover is now. Ken Ellaway had a small band and played there. He lived in Parkfield Place and when we got to our teens that was the meeting place for everybody. A quick game of snooker then off to the Plaza Cinema on North Road. We saw some good fights outside the Regal on Saturday nights between the Yanks and soldiers based at Maindy Barracks.

I went to St Joe's school and left in 1942 aged fourteen. We always had plenty of entertainment and the fields around our houses were a magnet for the show people such as Whites, Collins and Scarrotts.

Scarrots were well known for their boxing booth where the braver young lads would have a go. If they stayed on their feet for a round they would get a pound and a fiver for three rounds. If anyone got a fiver they really earned it. But it wasn't very often that they did. We had a regular visit from a man we knew as Professor Powsey. He would climb to the top of a 60ft scaffold, pull a sack over his legs up to his waist, set it on fire and dive into a water tank with a thin layer of oil on top which had been set on fire. The applause could be heard all over 'The Ranch' when he did his trick.

Owen Martin

A Quiet Wedding

I had a quiet wedding. I got married in St Martin's church. My husband was working for Gibbons the builders. If you took time off for a holiday you had no wages. You couldn't afford to stay home from work so we got married at eight o'clock in the morning. We had to do it because he would have lost his money. His mother made us a little do and afterwards we went for a walk around the park. Money was scarce in the 1930s. But we had a happy marriage. We were married for sixty-one years before he died.

Gladys Jenkins

Three Times A Day

My father was a preacher and on Sundays we were not allowed to play in the streets.

We could go for a walk in out best clothes and we used to go to the gospel hall three times on Sundays. They used to have Whitsun Treats and we looked forward to them as you would go on the back of a lorry to places like St Nicholas. You would have a bun, an apple and a bottle of pop and we thought that was wonderful. That was one time when all the family would meet and there were sack races for the children and that sort of thing.

Sylvia Kendrick

Street Traders

I remember the daily call of 'Milko' bringing the housewife, jug in hand, to the door for her measured milk. Drivers of horse-drawn vehicles shouting to their steads and cracking their whips at naughty boys swinging perilously behind. The fresh cockles man measuring his shellfish into our enamel bowls. Cycling errand boys whistling popular tunes and occasionally, down the middle of the street, a strolling minstrel rendering a trumpet solo or a tenor in a quavering voice singing *Rock of Ages* or a solemn hymn. Another entertainer was the hurdy gurdy man with his wizened, little flannel jacketed monkey.

Marcia Williams

Blocks of Salt

People would come around with big blocks of salt and they would carve off, with a saw, a great big lump and you would keep that for your cooking salt. The grocer's assistant would come down to the side door (he wouldn't go to the front door of course) and write down the order as well as delivering it.

Mrs John

Christmas 1947

Last year our Christmas party was held on Tuesday 16 December. Once again our hosts were the ladies and gentlemen of the staff of the Welsh Board of Health. The party was held at St Martin's Hall and our thanks are due to the vicar of St Martin's for allowing us to use the building. There were really two parties – one for the Infants and Standard 1, and one for the rest of the school – the one for the smaller boys and girls taking place first. We set out for St Martin's Hall at four o'clock. When we arrived we went upstairs to a large room where three long tables were laden with sandwiches and cakes of all descriptions. Soon we were seated and being served with jelly and blancmange.

After tea we went downstairs into another large hall with a stage at one end. We sat down and sang some of our

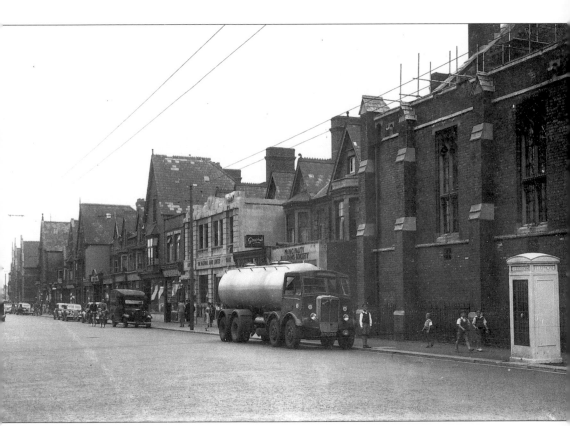

St Martin's church, Albany Road, c. 1936.

favourite songs. The curtain of the stage was pulled back to reveal a large Christmas tree, beautifully decorated. Then the conjuror appeared. He was a funny man and he performed some clever tricks. Ronald Rendall, Tony Cowan and Margaret Holland were invited onto the stage to help the magician with some very mysterious counting; and to try to tie knots in a piece of string. It was certainly an excellent turn.

Then the vicar took the stage. In a short speech he thanked all those who had worked so hard to make it such a lovely party – Miss Tovey, who was responsible for the organization, Captain Crawshay, the head of the Welsh Board of Health, and the Staff of that Department. We rounded it off by giving three hearty cheers. However the party was not quite over. Father Christmas put in an appearance, and how we cheered again! As we were leaving we received a present each.

We had had a most enjoyable time and were sorry that it had come to an end. As a little mark of our thanks Miss Tovey was presented with a writing case which had been made by some of the girls and boys of the school.

Aileen Lucas and Margaret Sidaway
(from Cathays National School magazine
Spotlight, *1947)*

A Lovely Life

Can you imagine a market garden stretching from Grosvenor Street, Brunswick Street, York Street and Lansdowne Road with glass houses? This is what it was like in the late 1890s. My grandfather, William Clark, was one of five brothers and one sister who left Langport, Somerset, in the late 1800s for Cardiff when the coal trade was expanding. Grandpa's brother George rented the land and Grandpa, Grandma and daughters moved to Grosvenor Street.

This was before the Lansdowne Hotel was built. The garden supplied two market stalls and vegetables to the ships in the docks. When York Street, Wembley Road and the bottom part of Grosvenor Street was built in the 1920s, Grandpa took land at the allotments which ran from Sanatorium Road to Leckwith Road and ran a smallholding. This was in the middle of the allotments and was back to back with another.

Grandpa had two fields, a small one for grazing and a large one for hay, which ran up to the fence around the hospital. The large field had a small pond which the cows would stand in, swishing their tails against the flies. The whole family was involved in the smallholding, as my mother, father, Aunty Francis and my brother and I would go there most days. There were cows, horses, a goat, dogs, cats, and most important, pigs. As children my brother Graham and I had a lovely life.

Dad had a large allotment and an apiary on the smallholding. His great interest was bee-keeping, which Mam shared. The fields were full of interest, the hedges a mass of flowers during the summer. And in the autumn there were blackberries for jam and elderberries for wine. At haymaking all the family would go to help and gather hay. Eventually all this finished when Broad Street was built.

Audrey Anderson

No Electricity

I grew up as a small boy in Richard Street, Cathays. The houses were terraced and comprise of three rooms – front room, middle room, kitchen and a single storey scullery attached. The hot water for the bath was provided by a gas geyser as electricity wasn't in supply. Cooking was mostly carried out by coal burning fires and ovens.

A stone shed across the bottom of the garden accommodated a copper boiler which was coal fired for laundry purposes. The shed also served as a coal bunker, bicycle store and carpentry shop.

The three bedrooms, each capable of holding double beds, meant that the middle rooms, downstairs and up provided a first home for most newly wedded couples. It also meant in many cases that the elderly were looked after and not farmed off to a home.

Jos Dwyer

Gramp and Grandma

My grandfather was a dedicated Salvationist born around 1840. He must have been one of the initial converts of William Booth. Gramp was the head of our household: a rugged, forthright working man, loving and honest as God. Anyone in trouble could come to Brother Morris and be assured that they would leave with a lighter heart.

If, at times, Gramp's pocket was also lighter, then it was no one's business but his own. Oh, you would have loved my Gramp. On my life, you would. Mind you, he was no push over. A typical martinet of the Army regime he ruled the family with rigid discipline. No strong drink, no smoking, no dance halls. Anyone daring to suggest a visit to the Canton cinema, an innovation then, was condemned for entering a den of iniquity. As for playing cards, if anyone of us were found with them then we held the devil in our hands. Now, when I am considerably older then he was then, I remember his angular body crouched over a huge coal fire, one hand curved to shield his face from the heat, and crooning his favourite Army hymns.

Grandma also was a hardy old veteran. She would suffer the most excruciating pain without a murmur. I've watched her soften her corns in soda water strong enough to take the hide off a bull elephant and then stoically scrape them with one of Gramp's rusty old cut-throats. I came across her one morning sitting on the side of the bed with her knotted old feet immersed in the contents of what is now discreetly termed a potty. Gran always called it a po! 'And you needn't look like that, my girl', she snapped. 'Finest cure for chilblains there is,' she said. No beauty, Gran, with her scragged-back hair and snapping black eyes. Her voluminous skirts never quite concealed the congenital deformity of one foot but under the worn black blouse, high-broached at the neck, beat a heart of warm compassion.

Gran couldn't read or write. She would sit of an evening at the scrubbed-white kitchen table and study the pictures in the War Cry by the dim glow of an oil lamp. At the age of seventy she qualified for a state pension and I qualified for the task of collecting it from the post office. She would mark her book with the requisite cross and with childish importance I filled

Mrs Phyllis Anderson, 1999.

in the back of the form as agent for the hand-out.

The money was a great help in those days because Gramp, the main bread earner, was in poor health at the time. Gran was a soft touch for halfpennies to us selfish kids but she had no patience with Gramp. Oh, she loved him and would minister to all his needs. And how! I remember the time when, for over a week, he suffered with a painful boil on his arm. All the hottest poultices slapped on by Gran proved of no avail. Finally she filled a bottle with boiling water; then, allowing it to cool a little, she tipped out the contents and placed the steaming opening over the area of the boil. For ten breath-held seconds Gramp endured it in silence, then

with a manical shriek he went down the garden path like a scalded cat. Oh the outrage on his features. I can see the old chap now, sitting on an upturned bucket at the end of the garden and staring wistfully into space.

Ah, those times! Coal fires and candlelight, the alarming pop of incandescent gas mantles, an innovation in our home. Indeed candles were an integral part of my childhood in the early part of this century. Of course gas was only installed in the downstairs rooms of our tall house. It cost precious pennies and a few people could afford to feed the greedy maw of the big red meter under the stairs. So, each night at bedtime, we kiddies would carry our candles wedged firmly in their enamel holders and Mam's voice would follow up the stairs 'Mind that grease, now! And blow it out the minute you're in bed.' For candles cost money and woe betide any one of us who wasted one inch. The threat of having to ascend those winding stairs in darkness filled our timid hearts with terror.

Yet it always seemed to be dark in the morning warmth of our heavily-curtained attic bedroom. But snug in the patchwork-quilted beds we would lie and listen to the clack of Gran's blacking brushes on the spit and polished kitchen range. She would be on her knees before the hearth, her only light a coal dusty-stub of candle waxed to a saucer on the floor.

Phyllis Anderson

Measles, Mumps and Chickenpox

It was routine, when I was young, for children to be encouraged to catch illnesses such as measles, chickenpox and mumps from others to avoid complications at a later age; so I in due course did this. There were no antibiotics then so that, for example, mumps took up to three weeks. When I discovered that at last I could swallow, I crept downstairs and took a stale crust of bread back to bed to chew. It was heavenly.

Geoff Bray

Wellington Street, Canton, 1964.

Live In Maid

My mother, right up until the time of the war, had a live-in maid and I grew up thinking that that was the sort of thing that would happen to me. I never expected that I would be the one to do all my chores and that sort of thing. It was a very big house we lived in with six bedrooms something like the houses in Cathedral Road. She always had somebody there to do the work. She was a very talented person. I've got all the pictures she painted. She could turn her hand to anything: embroidery, crochet, making clothes. She was such a clever woman, it was a hard act to follow.

Mrs John

The Allotment and Market Garden

As a young boy I used to accompany my father to his allotment at Leckwith. The plot was about where Broadhaven is now and, with many other plots, was watered in dry spells from two hand pumps. To get to the allotments one walked from the junction of Lansdowne Road and Grosvenor Street up a slight bank, across a railway level crossing and under the railway bridge. Between the railway crossing and the bridge were market gardens owned by a Mr Martin. This is where Lansdowne Avenue East and West are today. At the appropriate time of planting, many of the allotment holders obtained their plants from Mr Martin. Having passed under the railway bridge one saw The Lodge at the entrance to the

grounds of the Sanatorium, now Lansdowne Hospital, where children suffering from diphtheria and scarlet fever were treated in special isolation wards.

Henry Britton

An Old Toy Boat

During the last war, when my mother had to go to Llandough Hospital, my sister and me went to live with our maternal grandparents in Frederick Street. It was outside Canada House warehouse that my sister, Valerie, broke my collarbone by swinging me around and letting me go. She said we were playing fairies, but I couldn't fly, that's for sure!

Nana Donovan and Aunt Glad (she wasn't my aunt really) used to take me to the Central Cinema where I was introduced to Popeye the Sailor and The Three Stooges who I thought were hilarious. Neighbours would walk into my Nana's house just to find out the time.

My uncles, Philip, Billy and Jackie, all swam in the Glamorgan Canal and they used to dive under the water for the pennies thrown in by passers-by. On one glorious occasion they salvaged an old toy boat that happened to be drifting by and repaired and painted it for me.

When Grandpa died, in 1947, it was the custom then to lay-out the deceased in the front room of the family house. I was eleven years old and it was the first time I had seen a dead person. Naturally, I was upset and I remember my Uncle Jackie, a truly larger than life character, taking me out for a 'breath of fresh air'. We stopped at the canal bridge, around where Dillons bookshop (now Waterstones) is now, and watched the rats scurrying around the rotting vegetables that had been dumped there by the market stall-holders.

Brian Lee

One Huge Field

Before Viriamu Jones School was built in the 1920s, there was just one huge field which stretched back to College Road. Our house backed on to the school playground and when it was being built the night watchman was a kindly gent we called Grandpa Proctor. He used to bring us sweets and we loved him. When Western Avenue was built we went with the school to the River Bridge to witness Alderman Hill Snook declare the bridge open. There was a wide blue ribbon across the bridge which he cut and all of us kids cheered.

A piece of that ribbon was in a jug on my mother's dresser for years. The loch fields consisted of about five large fields with blackberry bushes and streams dividing each one. One of the fields had a well, which was fenced in, but the adjoining land was very boggy. Then there was Bluebell Wood which was a carpet in the spring and a popular place for courting couples. The allotments were beside the railway line and when we were in school on a fine day we could smell the pigs which were kept there.

To get to Llandaff Fields we had to walk through the loch fields alongside the canal, now Gabalfa Avenue, and through Treseders Nursery Gardens, now Glan Taf School, coming out by Hailey Park, then up alongside the River Taff and out through Llandaff Fields where we had the open air baths.

The lock keepers cottages were on the Glamorgan Canal bank along with the barge workshop which was adjacent to the Bluebell Woods. The Three Cups public house was also on the canal bank and many a drunk ended up in the canal. The loch fields are now occupied by Wickes and Staples. The only remaining works which were here before the war and are still here is British Ropes.

Joan Taylor

The Maypole

I remember going into the Maypole in town and a chap there was very clever with butter pats. He had these two pats, something like ping-pong bats only longer, and he could flip these around and make a lovely pattern on the butter. They also used butter moulds and they would fill this mould with the butter, press it down and you would have your butter embossed with a cow or a thistle or something like that.

The biscuits were not in packets they were in boxes with glass fronts and they would always give the children a nice biscuit as a good custom.

Mrs John

Basket Chair

A next door neighbour of mine was crippled. His legs hadn't grown from the knee down. He never went out of the house

Jim Cowley, 1999.

because he didn't want to be seen. But after the First World War there were so many cripples, as we called them, that he ventured outside in a wicker basket chair with two handles he had to push to make the wheels go around.

Gaynor Rosser

Sandwich Board Man

I remember Bert Jarvis who wore a battered top hat and carried a sandwich board. His hands were always well manicured and he was never without a large packet of Players cigarettes. Rumour had it that John Cory, the ship owner, occasionally gave him a pound note.

There was a woman nicknamed 'Penylan Sal' hopelessly drunk every Saturday night at the junction of Albany Road and City Road. Two policemen would usually lift her on to a small open truck and wheel her to the police station in Crwys Road. Then there was old Parry with a horse-drawn trap which had a boiler on the back emitting sparks as it made chips. He shouted 'Chips all hot and for a penny'. He lived in a whitewashed cottage in fields towards Penylan Hill.

A. Glyn Davies

The Candle King

I was born into a community which sadly we shall never see again. When you turned into Louisa Street from that river of life, James Street, you entered an almost self-sufficient world. On one corner was Wards, the butchers and greengrocers, a further yard on was the Edwards bake house where bread and rolls came up fresh every day.

Next door was the Candle King, the grocers: you name it he sold it! Halfway down the street on the same side was a house converted into a sweet shop at the front, latterly owned by a Mrs Beer, a resident of the street. On the opposite side to Wards was Charlie Alexander's bicycle repair shop. Charlie was a well-known cyclist throughout Cardiff and was the winner of many big races. He did a roaring trade with numerous errand boys' bicycles as well as seeing to many machines belonging to the dockers who nearly all rode their bikes to work in those days.

Near the shop was a little alleyway, where the bookies would take bets. It was

Clifton Street in the 1930s.

only two shops away from the well-known North and South public house run by Mr and Mrs Bryant, with Mrs Bryant being very much the boss of the establishment. There were no bookies or bookie's runners in her pub. The next two shops were T.G. Jones the butchers, and Tilkie the barber. Mr Tilkie, when cutting small boys' hair, used to sit them on a plank across the barber's chair to exercise what was known as a basin crop, the charge being four pence.

Halfway down the street was Dates, the printers, whose double doors at the end of their working day became the goal posts for our street football matches. Quite near was a firm of builders merchants called Ellis's.

All this in one small street, where many neighbours were related. There wasn't a fish shop in the street but that didn't matter, for twice a week Tommy Letton would trundle his barrow down from James Street. 'Come on ladies', Tommy would bawl, 'It's bargain time today, strictly Woolworths' prices only!' That meant there was nothing priced over sixpence and Tommy's fish, together with a few coppers worth of chips, would provide a dinner for the family. My Nana Maynard lived at No. 15, my Uncle Jack at No. 16, and we lived at No. 4, with my Uncle Bill next door to the Dates.

Quite near were the Williams and the Crabtree families, the Freemans and the Phelps, plus the Beer and Collins families. Other families that spring to mind were the Dites, the Harris family, the Cuddihys, plus the Bellameys and Amerys, the Radfords and the Pates, who had Norwegian backgrounds. Living close to each other were the Spanish folk, the Garcias, the Fernandez family and the Mazos. There were some fine looking girls amongst them

and Gloria Mazo gave me my first awareness that girls were something special when it came to looks.

I cannot leave my old street without returning to Mr and Mrs Bryant of the North and South public house. Mr Bryant spent hours in the cellar of the pub making beautiful steak and kidney pies. There was a grill in the pavement and we bike minding kids on a Saturday would gather like the Bisto Kids savouring the aroma. Mr Bryant would sometimes deliberately break up a couple of pies and pass the pieces on to us. Both of them were really good-hearted folk. Mrs Bryant would sometimes hire a coach for a day and take us to Barry Island or Lavernock or some other seaside resort. We looked forward to it for weeks beforehand and Mrs Bryant became known as 'Lady Bountiful'.

Jim Cowley

Walk To Buy Bread

We used to walk from Grangetown to Clifton Street on Saturday mornings just to buy bread. The single-decker tram fare was a penny, but this was probably the amount to be saved by not buying locally, so we walked.

Stanley J. Adams

Railway Accident

On the 12 August 1893, my father, Eddie Williams, his mother and baby sister were involved in a terrible railway accident at

Cardiff Docklands, once the heart of industry.

Llantrisant junction in which thirteen people were killed and fifty-seven injured. My father and grandmother were severely injured and his baby sister died later.

Len Williams

Cleaning Windows

From about the age of twelve my Saturday mornings were spent cleaning the ruddy windows for Mrs Mather, the newsagent in Tudor Road. I used to deliver the papers morning and evening and for that long task I earned four or five shillings a week.

Stan Sorenson

Heart Of Industry

My two brothers and I were born and lived in the very heart of industry. Since our birth we knew only of continuous sound. Lower Splott, the Dowlais cottages, was surrounded by the railway sidings of the Great Western Railway. They encircled us: steam locomotives shunting their wagons of coal to and from the docks and steelworks. The drivers whistles and toot to his latcher man, engaging and disengaging his train of wagons, the hiss of steam and the screech of iron wheels on iron rails, the clatter of buffers colliding continuously day and night: our lullaby of labour.

Just as near was the belching and bellowing of the blast furnaces of the Dowlais Steelworks, forging their iron ignots. The air thick with sulphur, soot and iron ore dust from the ever hungry coke ovens. The pollution and noise which assailed our ears and nostrils was, to us, Paradise. It was the oxygen, paradoxically, of our lives. South of us was the Bristol Channel and the docks. Twenty-four hours a day the explosions of the slag brought from the steelworks, and tipped into the sea at the foreshore reverberated through our little terraced house just hundred yards away.

Out in the Bristol Channel ships lay at anchor awaiting a berth in the docks, the crews eager for shore. Tugs and pilot cutters signalled their intention by toot, toot, toot then the long deep and clear reply of the ship's horn booming out. These sounds that were part of us, gave us comfort and was to our ears music.

Alan T. Grainger

Mr David John Jenkins (centre) celebrates his hundredth birthday.

These advertising hoardings were opposite the Tredegar Arms Hotel in Clifton Street, c. 1936

One Hundred and One

My father-in-law, David John Jenkins who lived next door, worked on the Taff Vale Railway. But later in life he took up optics and became an optician. He was always doing something, always busy, just like my husband. He lived until he was 101 and had all his senses.

Gladys Jenkins

Lighting Fires For Fourpence

I used to light the Jews fires for four pence. And that was wonderful wages then. They couldn't light fires on Saturdays because of their religion. We lived in Wood Street and it was like Jerusalem around there. I would go around again at twelve o'clock midday and bank the fires up again. And they would give me some Passover bread as well. I would collect my money on Sundays because they wouldn't handle money on a Saturday. I used to have a bag of pennies when I got back and my mother would be waiting for the money.

They used to leave some of these herrings in oil for me. I didn't like to say no. 'You eat them they will do you good,' they used to say. They used to call me Sipsy. I don't know if that's a Jewish word for little girl. Until I was about fourteen, I lit their fires and then my sister took over.

Maud Jones

CHAPTER 2

Childhood and Schooldays

Adamsdown schoolchildren, c. 1920.

Stanley Morris Sorenson

My name is Stanley Morris Sorenson. I was born on 23 September 1913. We lived in Pomeroy Street close to the Hamadryad Hospital. Not long after I was born we moved to Louisa Street where we stayed until I was about six years old before moving to Riverside. I was one of four brothers and two sisters. My schooldays were mainly at Kitchener Road. I enjoyed what schooldays I had. The teachers were excellent. Only one teacher I ever had objection to and that was Miss Davies who was rather sadistic in my view. I was expected to sit an examination to go to Canton High School. But the day I was due to do it I skipped to Leckwith woods and went bird nesting. I would have liked to have had a good education but when I left school I continued to teach myself. I was always interested in mathematics and geography and these interests were to stand me in good stead later on when I followed a seagoing career.

Stan Sorenson

Stan Sorenson, third left, back row, at Kitchener Road school, c. 1919.

The Italian Hot Chestnut Man

In my early childhood, the common way of getting from A to B was to walk. There were trams, but we only used those for urgent and longer journeys. A regular feature was a walk to town on a Saturday evening.

This is one of the ways children learned their way about, both literally and as to shopping and use of money. In the winter evenings I looked forward to reaching the City Lodge (St David's Hospital) for on the corner of Wellington Street there would be the Italian Hot Chestnut man. And I would probably be lucky enough to have a packet of these from his drawer inside the live fire in the body of his barrow. In the summer it might be ice-cream instead.

Reaching town (Duke Street hadn't been widened then and shops still stood between the castle and the roadway) it would be jammed full of pedestrians and how any horse traffic would pass I don't know. Even a cyclist had to dismount. The exciting moment was to reach Woolworths as all the shops remained open until 9 p.m.

Vince Jones

The Three Rs

I attended St John's Church School in Leckwith Road. As well as the three R's, the subjects included religious instruction once a week, the lesson being given by the curate or sometimes the rector. Also, the whole school, accompanied by the headmistress and the teachers, attended a weekly service in the parish church. The school bell was rung by the headmistress every morning and a hand bell for playtime in the yard. The National School, as it was known, was demolished some years ago and on the site stands a church hall.

Then, at the age of eleven, came an examination to enter Canton High School in Market Road. The headmistress was Miss E.C. Abott MA who lived in Penarth and she walked to and from Grangetown railway station along Tanyard Road, now Sloper Road. Discipline was strict, but schooldays were happy days. A play was usually performed once a year and this was enjoyed by the audience of pupils, parents and friends.

The girls' regulation uniform was a navy gym slip and blazer with a felt hat in the winter and a Panama hat in the summer. The school motto was 'Semper Sursum' and a hymn was usually sung in the hall before lessons commenced.

Ruth Hobbs

Heavy Caning

My elementary education took place in Virgil Street School, later known as Ninian Park School. The education provided basically a knowledge of reading, writing and arithmetic. Strict discipline and the frequent use of the cane was our lot; in a way that is unbelievable in the present age. The result of a heavy caning, six heavy blows on

The Cardiff Union Workhouse (City Lodge), c. 1905.

Ninian Park Road, at the junction with Leckwith Road, c. 1936. O'Dare's kiosk is on the left.

each hand delivered by the teacher as hard as he could, caused bruising and swelling for weeks afterwards. From Standard II, we had the same teacher, William Walter Coles, right through to Standard V. I particularly remember him and his class for the unique way in which he marked the daily register of attendance. Instead of calling out the pupils' names, we had to call out our own and the roll always started with me. He ticked them off until a silence indicated an absence and brought a stop to the sequence, whereon he would remark, so and so absent? Then the roll call would continue. After thousands of repetitions, the names of my classmates are permanently engraved on my memory: Adams, Aubrey, Butler, Bull, Carpan, Cooper, Crawley, Crosby, Davies, Fernley, Hancock, Hiles, Lawrence, Lewis, Lovering, Manson, Morgan, Muston, Maynard, Newman, Phillips, Plummer, Pritchard, Rodd, Salter, Shields, Thomas, Tugwell,

Saunders, Yearling, White, Wiseman, Roake, Coles, Marks, Pezzark, Jeremy. The list started off alphabetically originally, but additions to the class were just stuck on the end as they arrived. We have had several wars since then and many, to my knowledge are dead. In any case, those of us who are left will be following in due course.

Two headmasters I recall with appreciation. The first was Walter C. Jolliffe, who used to walk from school from his home in Partridge Road every day. He sometimes holidayed in France or Italy – not very common in those days – and on his return would give us talks about his travels. He was a good-hearted man who found time to give encouragement and practical assistance to pupils long after they left school. The headmaster who replaced him, was 'Major' C.J. Evans. Some years later I acquired a copy of the excellent history and topography of Glamorgan. This was compiled by a C.J. Evans and I never knew whether it was the same man.

Stanley J. Adams

A Book A Week

I went to Gladstone School until I was eleven years old then I went to Cardiff High School. I couldn't wish for a better school than Gladstone; probably because I had, for the four years I was in junior school, the best teacher anyone could wish for – Ernie Philips. In those four years I learned all there was to know about arithmetic and English. We read *The Old Curiosity Shop*, *David Copperfield* and *Black Beauty*. We had a library in each classroom and we were expected to read a book each week. We had to jot down in a pocket book the title, author, characters and a precis of the story.

Sometime during the following week we could be called upon to tell the class the story.

Jos Dwyer

Boys Brigade

I remember Jack Cox of Arran Street recalling, a few years before his death (he was then in his 90s), his membership in the 17th Cardiff Company of the Boys Brigade which was attached to Mount Tabor Primitive Methodist church in Moira Terrace facing Howard Gardens.

The Company catered for boys who lived in the surrounding streets of Adamsdown. Both the boys and the Company itself were poorly off financially and were unable to run a band. The weekly subs were only one penny, but not all could afford even this

Adamsdown school, 1924/25.

Jack Cox, fourth row from the back, third from the left.

small amount. Jack said that he could never remember paying his subs. Presumably this was covered by the Captain, who was Captain Bainton – a prominent member of the church and a former Army officer retiring with the rank of Captain.

Uniform consisted of a pill box cap, a haversack and a leather belt. Boys were expected to purchase cap and haversack and even this must have been difficult for the boys of poorer families. The belt was on loan and had to be returned to the Company on leaving. Jack recalled an occasion when his brother, Les, was in a spot of bother – a disagreement with one of the boys led him to throw his belt across the floor of the hall and then to storm out from the weeknight meeting. Jack and Les were brought up strictly by their mother who always had the cane ready hanging up on the back of the

kitchen door. On this particular occasion when she learned what had happened, she let into Jack, much to his surprise not knowing exactly what had happened. Chasing him down the passage, cane in hand, she ordered him to go back to the hall and to retrieve the belt, which the boys eventually did as the Captain was still in the church and hadn't locked up. Mother's retort was 'You leave the Boys's Brigade when I tell you and not before!'

Allen Hambly

Central Boys Club

We belonged to the Central Boys Club which was in Penarth Road at the time.

When the film *Boys Town*, starring Spencer Tracy, was showing in the Park Hall they gave us tin collection boxes and we stood outside the cinema collecting money which helped to build the Central Boys Club in Bute Terrace.

Philip Donovan

St David's Day, 1948

In school this year St David's Day was celebrated in customary fashion. The concert was a happy affair, a pleasing feature being the large number of children who took part. Many boys and girls were wearing daffodils and a few leeks were seen. The proceedings opened with the Welsh National Anthem and then the headmaster spoke for a few minutes. Five little plays were performed. *The Death of Llewelyn* was acted by Standard I. Anthony Fergusson took the part of Llewelyn; Barbara Green, the Queen; Mair Evans, a page; John Taylor, a soldier; Jack Goodall, and Michael Biddlecombe, Norman Soldiers.

Pat Johnson introduced *Griffith ap Cynan*. The story told how the brave Welsh chief was released from Chester Castle by Cynric Hir and taken back to his beloved people with great rejoicing. Trevor Edwards played 'Hugh the Wolf'; John Young, Prince Griffith; Robert Phillips, Cynric Hir 1st soldier Raymond Cook ; messenger, Keith Parkins ; jailors, Keith Colley and Colin Neathey; wife of Griffith, Cynthia Richards; Ladies-in-waiting, Marie Johnson, Maureen Gill and Joan Beasant.

The characters in *King Arthur's Cave*, performed by Standard III, were King Arthur, played by V. Salamon; Magician

Beryl Howe; Gwyneth, Joan Williams; Bronwen, Betty Thomas; Emlyn, Cecil Hagan; Dafydd, Mervyn Fergusson; Gwilym, Anthony Hughes; Mair, Marion Goodridge; shopkeepers, Robert Goodall and John Edwards; women, Glenys Davies and Kathleen Curtin.

Standard I's play was called *David and Paulinus*. The title parts were taken by Stephen Welch and Graham Hill, while other boys took parts of pupils. This little play told how David restored the sight of his teacher. It was written by Winifred Johnson, who spoke the introduction.

The play presented by Standards II and III was called *Caractacus in Rome*. Caractacus, the British Chief who had long resisted the Roman Armies in Britain was at last captured. His dignity and bearing so impressed the Roman Emperor before whom he was brought that the latter set him free.

A humorous sketch was performed by four girls of Standard II. Written by Muriel Neck, it was entitled *A Misfortune*.

The girls of Standard I put on choral verse speaking in three parts.

Between the plays musical items were given. Diane Mason played a piano solo. A group of songs was given by Standard III and IV with solo parts taken by Robert Rendall and Billy Greenslade. Several songs were also sung by Standard I and II.

Barbara Hancock
(from an article in Cathays National School's
Spotlight *magazine)*

Horse Shows

We came to Rumney, in 1937, to Ball Road (which was only a country lane then and

The Cardiff Horse Show was held in Sophia Gardens for many years.

now it is a vast housing estate). As a child I spent most of my time riding a pony. I went to Hywell Dda School in Ely and then to Rumney Central School. Later I went to Bloggs College and wore a royal blue and yellow uniform. It is now a nightclub opposite the New Theatre in Greyfriars Road. The discipline there was poor and I spent most of my time in the library reading magazines. We used to go to lots of the horse shows that were held in Cardiff. I spent lots of time going to the cinema and my screen idols were Errol Flynn and Robert Taylor.

Mary Jackson

John Toshack

During my early school days I went to school with Joan Light, the mother of John Toshack, the Cardiff City footballer. They also lived in Northhumberland Street in Canton. Incidentally, when John Toshack came to Australia to visit about twenty years ago, we invited him to our home for dinner.

Margaret L. Jones

My Walk To School

My home, Celyn Fach, is situated in Lake Road West opposite the park. I leave at ten past eight in the morning and have a long way before reaching the school. Sometimes I come across the field and occasionally I pick a few violets when they are in blossom. If I do not cross the field I come by the park. I pass many people on my way, some riding and some walking. Most of them are on their way to business. Many motorcars are about at this time in the morning, taking people to and from the town. The Roath Park is very large and it is divided into several parts. The part that I pass is that which contains the lake. At one end of this is a tower which was erected in memory of Captain Scott. Lately, a motor boat has been added to the many others which are there. After reaching the tram terminals I go along Shirley Road and call for a friend and then on to Roath Park School.

From a school essay written by fifteen-year-old
Ina Gale on 15 May 1915

A 1937 Dollar Tycoon

On this very important Saturday – the day I would know if the magical figure of a dollar (five shillings) could be achieved – I jumped out of bed, quickly dressed, only three articles of clothing (shirt, trousers and daps) and then downstairs into the kitchen. The little clock on the mantle piece showed 6.30 a.m. and I timed it just right. A quick wash under the tap in the outhouse and I was away, just three doors up to Edwards bakehouse where the big basket of hot rolls would be waiting for me. I knew Lou the baker would have a broken one smothered with butter waiting for me.

When swimming was allowed in Roath Park Lake, c. 1950.

I liked Lou, always cheery, and in his white singlet and trousers he always appeared cool; even though the heat in the bakehouse from those deep ovens seemed to envelope you as you opened the door, carrying with it that indescribable smell of baking bread. Lou wished me luck with my selling and off I went, staggered would probably have been a better word.

I wasn't very big for ten and the basket, even without the rolls, was big and awkward. The good thing was that if I had a good morning and sold the rolls quickly it would lighten. [I would go] out into the sunlight and begin the walk down Louisa Street towards Stuart Street, already the cry of 'Hot Rolls' coming from my lips. I'd never yet sold any in Louisa Street, but the call was automatic and you never knew your luck. Today my luck was in, Mrs Beer, who had a small shop in the middle of the street, bought half a dozen and I was sure now that this was a good omen for my ambition. This was further strengthened by two sales in Stuart Street and one in Dudley Street, before getting to Windsor Esplanade where the people with money lived and sales were expected to be good. Things went well for me and by eight o'clock I was back at the bakehouse with just six rolls left and after I paid in my money, Lou handed over my commission of one shilling and sixpence. Not much time before phase two came into operation. I put the money into the tin in my bedroom before running down the street to join the boys of all ages up to fourteen years who were waiting for the trams to start arriving with holidaymakers bound for the boat yard where Campbells passenger boats waited to take them over to Weston and Minehead. This was the most difficult part of my day to predict, hobbling – the

carrying of cases from the trams to the boat yard – depended on your ability to pick out passengers who would let somebody carry their cases for a penny or two. Also if you could judge the weight sufficiently to get it up on your shoulders or back in order to carry it the couple of hundred yards on a warm morning.

All in the hustle and bustle of discharging passengers and boys pushing and shoving in their efforts to attract the holidaymakers with their cries of 'Carry your bag Mister' with the bigger boys cuffing or kicking the smaller ones out of their way, if they looked like being successful while they went empty handed. Today turned out to be quite a good one, it seemed that more people were going to take a holiday across the Bristol Channel in this summer of 1937. Perhaps it had something to do with all this talk of Germany and somebody called Hitler wanting a war.

The thought was exciting, although I had heard my father telling my mother that no son of his would ever wear khaki because of experiences he'd suffered in the Great War. Experiences which had no doubt contributed to his death from consumption a few months before, but that was something else. Now it was back to meet more trams and more cases to carry until the flood of travellers ceased and it was time to sit in the warm sun and count the takings: one and tenpence, I'd hoped to make two bob, so that was disappointing. In addition, I was really hot and thirsty but I had no intention of spending any money today. Slowly I made my way back home. My Mam was still cleaning the offices of Mount Stuart Square but should be back soon and as I crossed the street to take up my position outside the North and South

Stuart Street, Cardiff Docklands, c. 1970.

Public House I thought how tired she always looked these days.

She was only tiny and I marvelled at how she coped with all those rooms at Empire House and with the washing she took in. However, some of the other boys had arrived outside the pub so I had to be on my toes. The art of minding bikes for the dock workers who left them in your care was to spot them as they rounded the corner and be the first in the race to meet them shouting, as you went, 'Mind Your Bike'. And because I was a fast runner, I always did well. One could never work out how well one would do because some of the dockers would be skint, when they finally left the pub, a combination of losing bets with the bookie's runner and a couple of extra pints leaving them to face the wrath of an angry wife, and a clip or a cuff for the bike boy helped give vent to their feelings.

By the same token a couple of successful bets might mean a silver thrummer though that wasn't very often. The one sure thing that my regulars 'Big Rusty' and 'Little Rusty' would give me tuppence each. They never failed no matter what drinks or bets they'd had. I often wondered why they were covered with rust and one Saturday had plucked up courage to ask why. They laughingly told me they spent all their time in a bilges of a ship with a lighted candle chipping away at rusty bulkheads. I still wasn't sure if they had been joking.

While I stood watching the bikes and talking to my mates, Little Alec came walking down the street carrying his case. He was the subject of much speculation in the docks being Jewish and a midget. Also there was a lot of whispering as to what he sold to the sailors who frequented the pubs in the docks area and that he was richer than anyone could imagine. Everybody

teased him and inevitably it ended with him taking a whistle from his pocket and saying he'd blow it and fetch a policeman. He passed by on the other side of the road, knowing full well that though he might go in every pub in the docks, Mrs Bryant would have none of that nonsense in the North and South.

As the shout of 'time please' came from within, the customers started to come on to the street and I collected my fees. Not bad at all, another shilling! A quick reckoning up made it four and four pence now.

But the misgivings began, if only I'd made two bob, I'd really fancy my chances, but that eight pence, that would take a bit of getting. When my mother had passed earlier, after her stint in the offices, she told me to make sure I came and had something to eat as soon as I'd finished. And the hunger pains were building up inside of me by the minute. But first I had promised my friend Ronnie that I would walk down the Big Windsor with him to make sure that Ron's brother Charlie got safely home.

Charlie was a character that everybody knew as 'Joe Beef' and on his way home from the pub he had developed the habit of diving fully clothed into the canal by the little locks and swimming to the other side. So for a few Saturdays now Ron and I had teamed up to take Charlie home to Clarence Place while trying to persuade him not to jump in. He always promised not to, but when the canal came into view the urge always overcame his good intentions. Like almost all docks people he was a capable swimmer and never seemed to suffer any ill effects. Today proved no exception and as usual Ron and I crossed the bridge and waited for him on the other side – half pulling and half dragging him

White Hart Inn, James Street, c. *1898.*

out of the water. Ron could handle it from here so I retraced my steps home for some food. It was really hot now so I decided to return to the canal for a quick swim after I'd eaten.

In addition to my treat of Saturday chips, my mother gave me some broken biscuits, bought cheaply from Candle Kings. I filled a bottle with water, put the biscuits in my pocket, and made the short journey back to the canal through James Street.

After a cooling swim, I ate my biscuits and drank the water before regretfully dressing and making my way back down James Street to West Bute Street. Soon the evening editions of the *Echo* would be delivered to the *Echo* depot in West Bute Street. A Mr Parker was in charge of the depot and he handed out the many dozens of papers to the accredited sellers: full-grown men who made what must have been a limited living from it. A few boys assisted the men, which in fact wasn't legal, but Mr Parker turned a blind eye to it and probably his own wages depended on the actual number of papers sold from the depot. Reggie Waldron was senior of the men who sold the *Echo*. He was slow on his feet and it was Reggie whom I helped, receiving two thirds of the commission for my efforts. As senior seller Reg was always the first to receive his quota. So quickly I took the agreed number from Reggie and ran my fastest towards Mount Stuart public house which by this time was open for the evening. It had the longest bar in the docks, was very popular and was easily the best selling point for the *Echo*, containing as it did the late racing results. Sales were excellent, but just as I was ready to leave, retribution arrived in the shape of the quickest of the men sellers and the cuff and kick I received almost knocked me off my feet. Fortunately a number of men in the bar shouted 'Leave the kid alone!' so I quickly made my escape.

By now the sellers were spread out around the pubs in the area and ten more papers still needed to be sold. So I made my way towards Smellys shop by the canal bridge. They were Italians and were recognized as makers of the finest ice cream in Cardiff. And on this lovely warm evening would attract custom from all over the city. I was confident that this was the spot to sell the remainder and so it proved. Within an hour they had all been sold.

St Monica's School, Cathays, c. 1950.

After paying Reggie, I was left with a grand total of a dollar and a penny. The penny bought a lovely thick wafer and as I made my leisurely way home the excitement was intense. Picturing my mother's face when I told her that for the first time for many a day the parcel would not need to be taken to the pawnbrokers at the beginning of the next week.

Jim Cowley

Hands Up For Boots

In school they used to keep boots in a cupboard for the poor boys. The master at Lansdowne Road School asked the class were there any of their fathers out of work. My brother put his hand up and the master told him 'Oh Keir, put your hand down. Your mother would be really embarrassed if she knew you put your hand up for boots'. But my father was out of work and my mother would have been glad of those boots for Alec.

Ruby Howe

Strict But Fair

I went to St Monica's School. The discipline was strict, but the teachers were very fair. Mr Smith was the headmaster. There was a Mr Lock, a Miss Davies, a Mr Green, Mr Ball and Mr Mathews. When I was in the junior class there was an odd character, Miss Emmys. She used to make up her face with rouge and her face looked like a clown's. She was very eccentric and

wasn't in the school very long. Rumour had it that she committed suicide by throwing herself off the cliffs at Penarth.

Tegwen Hugglestone

Gladstone School

In 1938 I started school at Gladstone, the school at the intersection of Whitchurch Road and Crwys Road. Built at the turn of the century it was, and is, solid and huge. My memories of Gladstone are in general happy ones, although on the first day, because nobody had said where the toilets were, I ran home at playtime for a quick relief visit. I soon told my mother that I did not want her to accompany me to school each day. My teachers during the infant years (five to seven) were Miss Stew, an unusual name, and Miss Humphreys, with whom I exchanged Christmas cards when she was over ninety.

Geoff Bray

Empire Day Concerts

I used to go to Gladstone School and my teacher in the last year was Miss James a very nice teacher. It was very good school and lots of the girls I still see around in the area. We used to have a concert on Empire Day and dress up. On one Empire Day we all dressed up as sailor girls. Some of the girls I remember are Mary Norman, Delphine Brewer, Betty Royal, Margaret Chamberlain, Valerie Navard, Mildred Gibbon and Catherine Jones.

Marion Jenkins

Gladstone schoolchildren, St David's Day, c. 1940.

Empire Day concert, Gladstone School, c. 1948.

Don't Tarry Sell To Harry

Cathays, in those days and for the whole of my childhood, was a static community with little change and everybody seemed to know everybody else, and everybody else's business too. I suppose it was in our area mainly lower middle class [people] – tradesmen, clerks, shopkeepers – and few of the women worked. The streets were empty of vehicles. I don't think anyone had a car, and the long era of horse and cart was not yet at an end. No doubt the rationing of petrol during and after the war extended this. I recall the horses bringing around the milk carts with churns, not bottles, [and] the rag and bone man Harry Parfitt: 'Don't Tarry sell to Harry' and the knife sharpener on his bicycle, the French Johnny Onions, Mr Burgess selling fish, and other street vendors.

The iron pillar to which the horse's reins were attached still existed in 1993 at the corner of Lisvane Street but the cobbled area has long gone. At the corner of Rhigos Gardens Lane a tiny dairy, Jacks, was situated in what is now a house garage. Above the door somewhat incongruously was a fine painting of cows in a country scene. The streets were then safe for children to play. Each street had a corner shop and children were frequently called from play to go to the shop. Houses, of course, did not have refrigerators only larders and cold slabs, so purchases were made daily. Everybody received their pay in cash weekly, and purchases were therefore in cash or on short-term credit. Few people had cheque books, and credit cards were not invented until many years later.

We were frequent shoppers at the Co-op and to get the annual dividend payment you had to quote your number when purchasing. I still remember ours, it was '6769'. It must have been a mammoth task to calculate the dividends for the thousands of regular customers in those pre-computer days.

Monday was washday and every garden had lines full of washing on that day each week. There were of course no washing machines or spin dryers. We had a wash house, which the modern generation now call a utility room, with a copper cylinder, a wooden stick and a mangle, which I used to turn if I was at home.

Geoff Bray

Model Railway

I was very keen on model railways. Very fond of them and I had a set for Christmas. It was regularly extended if you know what I mean with extra rails and locomotives. It was made by Bing, a German company and the company still exists by the way.

John Attree

Knitting and Sewing

In the infants we learned to knit on fine steel needles with tough stringy cotton. In the upper school we knitted woollen scarves for the Tommies in World War One. We learned to sew on four inch squares of stiff, white calico and each stitch had to be of regulation length and evenly spaced or unpicked. By the time I finished my Persil white sample it was a mere smudge of grey rag measles spotted with my life blood from needle pricks.

Before long we were sewing sandbags for the war effort. At the end of each school year

A young John Attree with his model railway.

the top girl in each class received a document, Bacons Excelsior Regulation Ladder. It was a ladder of flags bearing a pupil's name and end of term marks. The ladder for Standard IB in 1913 had fifty flags with the names of those who hadn't made it on the steps below indicating a class of sixty children. Although classes were large there seemed to be few disciplinary problems. Small wonder for we had to sit with our hands behind our backs for most lessons. We sang to the teacher's hand signals. Her clenched fist thrust forward meant doe. We chanted spelling and multiplication tables daily and they still echo in my mind. Especially twice twelve is twenty-four shut your mouth and say no more.

Marcia Williams

Plain, Dumpy and Kind

I was in the junior school at Kitchener Road and my teacher was Miss Payne. In those days each class had but one teacher and she taught everything. Surely a teacher who does that is more educated than teachers who specialize in one subject. Miss Payne was plain, dumpy and kind. But when I discovered she was actually a Guide Captain, she became beautiful in my eyes. How I envied the more fortunate girls in my class whose parents could afford the uniform to be a Guide. She also planned trips to the sea in the summer holidays. It seemed an ordinary adventure after a while. I remember asking Mam if she had ever seen the sea. She stood still for a moment and looked pensive. 'Yes, I believe so,' she told me. 'I went to Weston for my honeymoon. It was to be a week, but we came home on the Tuesday.' Seeing my puzzled look, she added, 'I was homesick'.

One school day morning Miss Payne took the whole class to the museum. Knowing we would be required to write an essay on this venture I carefully scrutinized every picture, every statue and listened to the explanation from her learned lips. Finally we entered the Welsh kitchens. The bedroom puzzled me; the patchwork quilt, the wooden cot. Standing with my nose pressed against the glass my excitement waned. An inexplicable peace warmed my heart. I knew that Welsh dresser; I knew the blackened pot hanging in the large black cavern of the fireplace, the flag stoned floor, the warming pans on the white-washed walls. I was called to task the following day for my description of things in that kitchen that were not there. 'Are your folks Welsh?' I was asked. 'I don't know Miss,' I told her. 'Well, never mind' and as I was turning away she added kindly, 'It was a very good essay, nevertheless.'

Phyllis Anderson

A Real Character

Nearly fifty years have passed since I left St Peter's Roman Catholic Secondary Modern School which used to be in St Peter's Street off City Road. A block of flats now stands where I used to play in the school playground. The same playground that used to get flooded in the centre every time there was heavy rain. On one occasion my best friend Ronnie Morgan pushed me in it. Still, I had the last laugh as the teacher sent me home to dry out! The teachers I recall are Jack Hegarty, the headmaster, Jack Lane,

Jack Sharkey, Tom O'Reilly, Dennis Donovan, Chick Fearbee, 'Nobby' Francis and Frank Callus. One of them, I won't say who, had holes in the heels of his socks which caused us great amusement. His favourite saying was, 'As true as God made little apples'.

A real character was teacher Ossie Lord. If you did well he would give you a piece of paper with the word 'Good' written on it. Then if you misbehaved, and you had to have the cane, you would give him this bit of paper, and you would get off scot-free. One classmate, I believe it was Tony Verallo, was quite an expert in forging these 'goods'.

Another classmate, John Sullivan, saved up a tobacco tin full of 'goods' only to have them pinched from his desk. The saddest day I remember was when one of the teachers called the class together to tell us that one of our classmates, his name was Jimmy McDonald, had drowned while playing in the docks at a place known as the Timber Floats.

School fights were regular happenings and many a fisticuff I had in the lanes of either Bedford Street or Richmond Road. The funny thing is I can't remember what started them. The word would get around that there is a fight down the lane after school and surrounded by a gang of blood lusting youngsters we would scrap until one or the other had a bloody nose which usually ended the contest.

The long, dark smelly air-raid shelter in the playground was a place to be feared. The 'big boys' would make us run the gauntlet, so to speak. We would be hit about the head by the boys who would be hiding as we were forced to dash through one end and out the other.

Brian Lee

St Peter's Roman Catholic School, Class I, c. 1942.

Transportation Threat

As a child, I remember being caught by a verger climbing over the wall between Llandaff Fields and the churchyard of Llandaff Cathedral, and threatened with transportation. There's a grim folk memory for you!

Stanley J. Adams

Love and Hate Situation

Schooldays were a love and hate situation. When the bell rang for going home it was sometimes a great relief. The shouting and bawling, the occasional clip across the ear, and the inevitable cane – six cuts were always a threat – so you did look forward to getting out and having some fun. Schoolboy fun in those days was a mixture of marbles in the gutter, leap-frog up against the wall, football in the streets and cricket against the lamp-post and tying house knockers together – Rat, Tap, Ginger.

Ron Davies

A Moorland Road Boy

In that granite temple of learning,
Where we dreamt of success every day,

It had nothing to do with lessons,
But everything to do with play.

The trophy lined corridor seemed endless,
With pictures adorning the walls,
Of teams in peppermint jerseys,
And captains holding footballs.

Oh! How we longed to be chosen.
A game in the seconds would suit.
Or perhaps we could carry the lemons,
Maybe even dubbing the boots.

Perchance at Splott Park we'll be favoured,
To mind trousers, coats and school caps,
Until the final whistle is sounded.
And they change from their boots to their daps.

Kitchener, Radnor, Windsor Clive,
They never would give up.
Always a constant challenge,
For the William Seager Cup.

Adulation our heroes surrounded,
To us they deserved our acclaim,
For the one thing they all had in common,
They played for the joy of the game.

Edward J. Kendrick

Famous Face Flannel

I am not sure of my earliest memory – I think however it may have been of my mother washing my face with me trying to catch the flannel in my teeth! If we were having a picnic or other outing she would produce a damp flannel from a spongebag to wipe the chocolate or ice cream remains from our faces.

Geoff Bray

Moorland Road School soccer team, 1922/3.

CHAPTER 3

Working Life

General cargo ships in Queen Alexandra Docks, c. 1948.

'Tubby' Alexander

I worked for Charlie 'Tubby' Alexander, cycle agent, after the war at 25 James Street, on the corner of Louisa Street. I worked there for nine enjoyable years from 1946 to 1955. Charlie's father William – we all called him Pa – was a nice old chap and one of the old school and a real character. Apparently he served in the Boer War and

spoke Afrikaans. He was very religious, always quoting the Bible. He was a ship's pilot prior to starting a small cycle repair shop in the Dowlais Arcade in West Bute Street. Charlie was nicknamed 'Tubby' because he put on weight while serving in the RAF in the war. He was stationed at Boscombe Down RAF Experimental Station as an engineer. On demobilization, Charlie built up the cycle business which survived

Charlie Alexander who cycled 13,000 miles annually.

Donald Williams in 1953.

until the redevelopment building programme of Cardiff Docklands and surrounding areas.

Charlie and his father were both likeable characters. Charlie always wore plus fours, a jumper, long woollen socks and Reg Harris cycling shoes. Once a year he would make an exception when he donned his brown demob suit for cycling club dinners and the annual coach trip to the Cycle Exhibition at Earls Court in London. Charlie was well read, good at history and spoke very good French. This proved to be quite useful when serving the many Johnny Onion men who came over from Brittany and would frequently call in the shop for urgent repairs. There was nothing Charlie didn't know about bikes and cycling. He was a man for all seasons, never put off by the weather and

he clocked up around 13,000 miles a year by racing and club riding at the weekends. He held many records in his heyday in the 1930s and worked with a single-minded purpose and dedication to cycling and all that went with it having been a member of the 100 Miles Club all his life.

There were four of us at Charlie's directly after the war, including Charlie and his father. Cliff Smith, a buddy of my uncle John, was a member of the Byways Road Cycling Club. He started with Charlie after being demobbed from the RAF. Cliff was a flight engineer on Wellington bombers and had the distinction of being a member of the Goldfish Club. This honour was only given to aircrew who had to ditch in the sea while on a mission.

I was bottom of the pecking order and the youngest. Between us we could satisfy most customers whether it was for repairs to bikes, motorcycles or made to measure solid tyre replacements for push chairs. I recall regularly repairing the Cardiff Corporation band's drum major's mace by removing the dents in the silver knob. He was quite skilled throwing it up, but on occasions gravity got the better of him. I also remember having to weld up cracked typewriter bases for Duncan McConnell at the Typewriter Services Ltd opposite our shop. Our work ranged from repairing punctures to building made to measure racing bikes and we enjoyed every minute of it. It could be said that these were my most impressionable years and probably the most educational period of my life, as a result of meeting so many different kinds of people.

Some of them were policemen and I remember Viv Brooks a well-known policeman from Bute Street police station. I remember him and his colleagues visiting the shop with lists of stolen bikes. Most of the local people would call in the shop for mundane items such as Three-In-One oil for the sewing machine or a tin of gloss enamel for home use. Two of the local schoolboys, Alan Porter and Eric Freeman, of Louisa Street would hang about the workshop. Their parents always knew where to find them at meal times.

There were many regular customers who spring to mind: Dimitri Kaloqeras, Jim of Kristensen and Due, Fred Saddler the

A sketch of Charlie Alexander's cycle shop as remembered by Don Wiliams.

Harry Ferris in 1932.

tobacconist next door, Tilke the barber with his collection of shaving mugs and ships in bottles, Tom and George of T.&G. Jones the grocers, Joe Malfatti, of the Cabin Café in Stuart Street and, of course, Jim Cowley the Dockland writer from Louisa Street.

Donald Williams

Lloyd George

Harvey Harris was, to my mind, the doyen of photographers. He was the chief photographer at the *Western Mail & Echo* when I started work in the process department. One day he asked me what I was doing on Saturday and I told him I wasn't doing anything. 'Right', he said, 'you can come with me to see Lloyd George; he's in Llandridod Wells'. It was a terrible day and when we got there it was pouring with rain. I'll always remember, I carried his camera bag. There were all these London photographers there and when one of them saw Harvey he said, 'Thank God, here's Harvey'. Harvey said, 'What's the matter?' and one of them told him, 'He won't come out'. Harvey said, 'Leave it to me'. There was a police inspector there and he told Harvey that he couldn't go in the house. Harvey told him to tell Lloyd George that Harvey Harris wanted to see him. Well, the police inspector came running back and told Harvey he could go in. So Harvey knocked on the door and a gruff voice said 'Come in'. We went in and there sitting at a table was Lloyd George. He was absolutely mad; I can see him now. He said to Harvey, 'You can clear off, I'm not doing any

photographs. I'm not doing anything'. Harvey said to him, 'Look David', he called him David! 'You have got your job to do and we have got ours. Outside there are twenty-five photographers who will have an awful time with their editors if they don't get their pictures.' So in the end Lloyd George said, 'Alright, I will give you two minutes'. So we went outside and these fellows were overjoyed. We could have had anything we wanted off them after that.

Harry Ferris

Dressmaking

I did a bit of dressmaking in Marments – till they sacked me because I kept stepping on this poor woman's feet. I was only picking up pins and all these little bits and pieces of material.

Maud Jones

Second Hand Clothes

My grandmother used to buy and sell second hand clothes. I would go with her to Minehead and Ilfracombe. We would travel on the bus or tram to the docks and then go on the white-funnelled boats. She would deal with all these people who lived in beautiful houses. She would send them a postcard and then they would have all these clothes in heaps around the room. She would buy in 'lots', as we called it: shoes, hats and so on all went in canvas bags and the cabby would come for us. My grandmother always wore black and when

On 25 March 1902 the first electric tramcar left the new tram depot at Newport Road.

she was selling she always wore a black apron with a huge pocket in the front where she kept the money.

Clarice Langdon

20th Century Fox

I worked, from 1938, for 20th Century Fox Films in Dominion Arcade in Queen Street as an assistant despatch clerk. We worked in the cellars under the arcade with the film repair girls. Our job was to despatch the films to the various cinemas by means of the vans of the Film Transport Service which had its garage next door to the old tram depot at Newport Road. In Dominion Arcade were 20th Century Fox, Pathé,

General Films, Warner Brothers, First National and Columbia. Many times I had to carry films from the arcade to the projection box of the Empire. I worked from eight o'clock on the Sunday morning until two o'clock on the Monday for the princely sum of 2s 6d checking that the films were being correctly sent to the cinema.

A. Knighton

Lord Glanely

I worked in offices at Cardiff Docks from 1917 until 1924 and again in 1939 until 1950. I clearly remember Lord Glanely's two horses entered in the 1919 Derby and they were Dominion and a rank outsider Grand

Parade ridden, I believe, by Tommy Weston. Glanely, who had offices in the docks, told everyone that Dominion, without any doubt, would be the winner. A big Exchange sweepstake was formed with tickets costing a guinea each. Grand Parade won at 33-1 and Glanely was not very popular for a while with the lot who had backed Dominion. There was a stockbroker who was so mean he would never throw away a piece of string or brown paper. He had to undergo an operation in Llandough Hospital. A man who was sorry for him offered to take him there in his car and even collected him when he was discharged. The stockbroker was so profuse in his gratitude, he sort out his benefactor a few days later and said I have a gift for you. The gift was a bunch of home grown mint and when the stockbroker died he left £250,000.

A. Glyn Davies

Hand Loom Weaving

I went to work in the Gripolly Mills in Sloper Road. I was doing hand weaving for nineteen years. I was the first one to weave nylon in Cardiff. They bought a German loom and they put it down and no-one could work it. So I had a little go because I'm machine mad. They said, 'Go down to the laboratory', and I was there for ages and I found out how to do what they wanted. Later I went to London to work in Marconi's, doing government work and I was working in a locked room because it was all to do with the war effort.

Maud Jones

Pulling the Toffee

The Popes have been in business since my grandfather's time. I'm not sure when he started but he had a sweet shop in James Street down the docks. And somewhere around about 1905 he opened another shop in 227 Cowbridge Road which is now a bookies. He ran that shop up until just before the war, when he retired. We used to get old people coming in a few years ago. Of course they are gone on now. But they used to say how, as children on their way to school, [they would] stop and look in the window of the old sweet shop to see my grandfather pulling the toffee which they did in those days. And he used to make his own sweets. My father started the photographic business just developing and printing in 1924. My grandfather gave him a small part of the shop to start. He was only there about twelve months and then the opportunity came for him to buy our present premises Popes Photo Services at No. 235 Cowbridge Road. My father bought this shop from Barclays in 1925 and we have been here ever since.

Dennis Pope

Fifty Years In Films

My father, John Blagden, worked for the Rank Organisation for more than fifty years. He started off as a projectionist and also graduated to doing the stage lighting and special effects for various shows. He worked at the Empire, later known as the Gaumont, the Odeon, the Capitol and even the New Theatre at one time. He met many famous film stars and show business people: Laurel

A.W. Pope, confectioner, at 227 Cowbridge Road East, c. 1906.

Dennis Pope and his daughter Deborah, 1998.

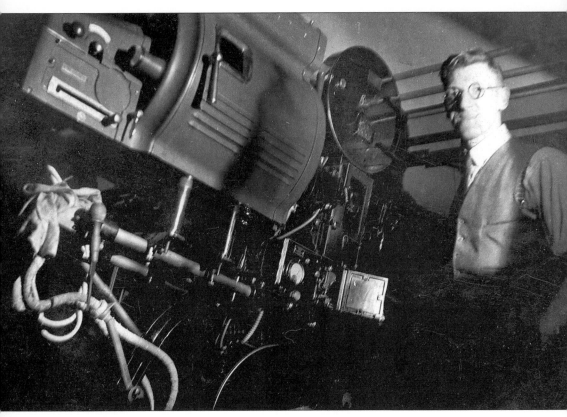

John Blagden, c. 1950.

and Hardy, Cary Grant, Montgomery Clift, Bill Haley and Cliff Richard to name but a few. But the one who made the biggest impression on him was Jack Buchanan who he said was a lovely man – a real gent. I have all their autographs in a book he gave me.

Meg Johnson

Four In Hand

In 1935 any boy of fourteen who was suddenly offered the chance to start work in a brewery did not take many moments to make up his mind that he wanted the job.

But when it became known that the place of work was also the home and workplace of brewery dray horses in Crawshay Street it was only a matter of 'When can I start?' As the office junior I was called upon to take messages, files, etc, to various departments such as the Transport office, Aerated Water department, Wine and Spirit stores and others none of which were anywhere near the stables.

This did not deter me from calling on them either going to or leaving my destination. Apart from the stabling, where the horses were kept, you could find the mess room for the dray men which was combined with the harness room. On the walls would be the prize winning rosettes and certificates which had been won by the horses at various agricultural shows. Names of some of those involved with the greys include: David Humphries, Syd Thompson, foremen Ted Robinson, Harry Phillips, Harry Webb, Syd Tudor and Dick Snow.

A sight to behold was a pair of greys, or four-in-hand, as four were known, leaving the brewery premises at Crawshay Street and turning left into Penarth Road at a steady trot before breaking into a gallop to meet the rise on entering St Mary Street to commence the day's deliveries to licensed premises in the city. Another recollection is the occasion when the *Cinderella* pantomine was at the New Theatre. The six little white ponies which drew Cinderella's coach across the stage needed stabling and where else than to join the famous dray horses at Hancocks Brewery. An enthralling sight was that of the massive figures of a grey looking down at the diminutive figure of one of the panto ponies in the adjoining stall.

Harry Welchman

Sue Lawley

In 1969 I had an invitation to attend the *Western Mail* centenary celebrations at the London Savoy Hotel. The do was in the Savoy and I stayed in the Waldoff. I went up with Syd Graves, the chief librarian, and we shared a room. As we were dressing there was a knock at the door and a girl came in wearing a beautiful gown. She was one of the hostesses who worked on the paper. She asked would one of us gentlemen be kind enough to zip up her gown as she couldn't do it herself. She said, 'Thank you very much, I'm Sue Lawley'.

Harry Ferris

My First Job

When I left school in 1952 I went to work at Guest Keen & Nettlefolds steel works. I worked in the Instrument Department and

The Hancocks greys, c. 1935.

GROSS EARNINGS		2	14	8
HOLIDAY PAY				
HOLIDAY FUND				
TAX REFUND				

57	994 LEE B. J.								
NAT. INS.	HOL.	Savings	Spts.	Sick Club	Man. Hse	Acc. Ins.	CWN Club		TOTAL
2/10½	8			5					3 9

TAX DEDUCTION			
TOTAL DEDUCTIONS		3	3"
NETT EARNINGS			

| PAY | | 2 | 1 | 4 |

IMMEDIATELY AND BEFORE OPENING

See that this Packet Contains the Correct Amount.

No claims for shortage will be admitted AFTER this packet has left the Window.

G. K. N. Form No. 141.

Brian Lee's first wage packet, 1951.

my boss Horace Jenkins, whose mother kept a herbalist shop in Bridge Street, told me that he had been in school with my father. Every other day or so I had to put water in the radiator of his car and I still remember the licence plate number which was CUH 624.

As well as running errands for the instrument mechanics, I had to go around the factory changing all the charts and filling the various instrument's pen holders with red or green ink. Honeywell Brown and Clark instruments come to mind. For just seven pence I could have a three-course meal in the works canteen. The first week I took home £2 1s 4d ½ and I still have my first pay packet. Later I was sent on an Adjustment to Industry course at San Pierre,

Chepstow, which is now a well-known golf club. We stayed in this mansion for four days, but I cannot remember what we did there, apart from play records. One which was called something like *Oh How Loves He Cooks The Meat* I have never heard since! I was later given some sort of a mechanical test to see if I had what it took to become an apprentice, but I failed it miserably.

Brian Lee

Piece Of Paper

I went for an interview for a job with the Western Mail & Echo. When I got there, there were about twenty to thirty others waiting in the corridor. Anyway, when it got to my turn they called out my name. I walked in and on the floor was a piece of paper so I picked it up and put it on the table. One of the interviewers, Pop Rickards, asked me a few things then he looked at the other three people who were doing the interviews with him and said, 'He will suit me I don't want to see anyone else.' He told me that fifteen people before me had walked into the room and walked over that piece of paper. He said he wanted somebody tidy in the job I would be doing and that's how I got the job.

Harry Ferris

High Heels and Peep Toes

I started work at Marcus Goldblatt's shoe shop in Frederick Street at the age of fourteen. We made high heels, peep toe and

Ely Paper Mills Institute, Ely, c. 1936.

To the left of picture is the Western Mail & Echo offices on St Mary Street.

Workers at Marcus Goldblatt's shoe shop, Frederick Street, c. 1950.

Joan Burnell (née Goodall) wearing a v-neck jumper with her workmates, c. 1951.

lots of wedge heeled shoes and real fur boots. The factory later moved to Penarth Road and then later on to Maes-y-Coed Road. But unfortunately after a few years the company went bankrupt.

Joan Burnell

Trolleybuses

My father, Jim Stone, was in charge of the first convoy of trolleybuses to Cardiff. He had to map out a route from Blackweir, making sure that there were no low bridges or other hazards. My father worked for Cardiff County Council Transport for forty-seven years, starting as a cleaner in Roath Depot when he was a young man. He was away serving in France in the 1914-18 war and then returned to his job, finally ending up as district inspector in charge of Sloper Road Depot.

He had many interesting tales to tell, not least the time he was fined for exceeding the speed limit at seventeen miles per hour on solid tyres in Mackintosh Place. The reason for his haste was that, at that time, there was also a private bus company operating on the same route and he was racing to reach the next stop first to capture the passengers.

Barbara Stone

Portmanmoor Road

Ran the road iron ore dusted,
Tramway laden, North to South.
Hefty dockers and Spillers maidens,
Heading for the dockyard's mouth.

Stooping housewives burdened under
Edgar Bryon's King Edward spuds.

District Inspector Jim Stone at his Sloper Road office.

Edward J. Kendrick, c. 1937.

Bags of flour from Archie Saunders
For the navvies favourite puds.

Trimmers homeward bound are wending,
Shovels on their bikes are tied.
Sirens from the docks a'sounding
Readiness for the evening tide.

Underneath the Lombardian Trinity,
Harry Clompus plied his trade.
Ma Waites, Fishes and Irelands,
Sold Woodbines and lemonade.

Lardy cakes from Wilmots,
Magees for gravied pies.
Gregors for fish and chips,
Solly Joseph for shirts and ties.

Wide were accents ranging,
From India to Donegal,
While the smoke and the dust from the
steelworks,
Showered its blessing on one and all.

Edward J. Kendrick

Queen Mary

When I worked for the Great Western
Railway I saw Queen Mary when she came
to Cardiff. Because of all the old stone
steps at the station they decided to send
her down in the lift. Well, the only lifts
they had were for the goods which were
mostly fish. So they scrubbed and scoured
this one lift and put a wooden chair
belonging to the railway in it. I can see her
now sitting bolt upright with her umbrella
in her hand.

Gaynor Rosser

M.V. *Holmside*

When I left school at fourteen I went to
work for an engineering company in the
docks. Later on I went to sea, just like my
father. In due course I obtained my second
mates certificate then my first mates
certificate and finally, in 1946, I had my
masters certificate. My first ship as captain
was the *Empire Seaman*. One ship I watched
being built in Aberdeen, in 1959, was the
Holmside owned by the Burnett Steamship
Company, Newcastle-on-Tyne, and which
I captained in the 1960s.

Stan Sorenson

Boy With A Butterfly

Later on I went to work for Cardiff
Corporation Parks department and at
various times I was based at Ely Racecourse
recreational grounds, Victoria Park,
Thompson's Park and a few other parks
besides. Thompson's Park, with its well-
known Boy with a Butterfly statue, was
certainly a pretty park in the 1950s, when
I was given the task of weeding the garden
paths.

Even for a young lad it was back-
breaking work, but it was a pleasure to be
working in the outdoors in the sun. Young
mothers pushing their high prams – you
don't see many prams like that today –
their infants shaded from the sun, would
stop and talk. My supervisor was a man
called Jack Lewis and although nearly fifty
years have passed I can still remember the
ticking off he gave me for sweeping out our
wooden hut without sprinkling water on
the floorboards first. The trouble was he

Captain Stan Sorenson and his wife Eileen aboard the MV Holmside, c. 1960.

M. V. HOLMSIDE
Owners- The Burnett Steamship Co. Ltd.
Newcastle - on - Tyne.

MV Holmside, *owned by the Burnett Steamship Co. Ltd.*

arrived at the hut to have his sandwiches only to find the place in a cloud of dust.

Brian Lee

A Reserved Occupation

After leaving school I attended a commercial college in Roath. My first job was as a shorthand typist at William Lewis & Sons, Coach Builders & Engineers. I remained in that position throughout the war years, as it was considered to be a reserved occupation, as we were doing work for the different Ministries of Government.

I worked there for eight years. When I married, I left their employ as in those days women were not expected to continue their employment.

Margaret L. Jones

Out Of Work

Work and money were both scarce. When my father was out of work for six years we moved from a big house in Moorland Road to a little cottage in Tenby Street. I remember the day my father got a job because he cried. My father had been all

The Boy with a Butterfly statue, Thompson's Park.

Monica Walsh (far right) with two of her collegues, c. 1956.

round the world and had roughed it everywhere. It was a poignant moment for me and all the family.

Edward J. Kendrick

Leather Business

My grandfather was Lewis Edwin Coles. He had a leather business which started in Wyndham Arcade and then later moved to a warehouse in Bridge Street. When he passed away the business was taken over by my father Harry Edwin Coles and his brother Albert. They carried on the business for many years afterwards, passing the business down to my own brother, Alan Coles, years later. The warehouse was demolished with many other buildings to make way for a new road that was being built. My other brother, Lewis Coles, went into the pharmaceutical world and eventually became President of the Association of Public Analysts. He gained his Doctorate in chemistry at the University of London.

Margaret L. Jones

Hopkin Morgan Bakery

I joined Hopkin Morgan Bakery as a junior clerk in 1946 straight from school and we were then situated on the North Road junction with Western Avenue and next door to the Leyland Motor Company. We were a hard working friendly group of people from the bakers and dispatch workers, to the delivery men and office staff. The horses' stables were in the backyard along with a few electrically-driven vans. We all worked long hours and I can remember on Bank Holiday Saturdays and Christmas Eves being there until almost midnight, unpaid overtime, and waiting for the drivers to pay-in their cash and balance their books. It wouldn't happen these days would it? We also had many happy times on the annual outings to places such as Stratford on Avon and it was quite sad when around ten years later the place was demolished to make way for the Gabalfa fly-over and the staff were transferred to other areas. I myself went to head office in Park Grove Cardiff, where I worked for a further ten years before the business of this office was moved to Bristol. There are however still five of us from the Park Grove office who still meet every two weeks and have done so for the last thirty-three years which must be a record!

Monica Walsh

CHAPTER 4

Leisure and Entertainment

Members of the Cathays Terrace Embassy Skating Rink Club, 1951.

Up In The Gods

Today when you go to the cinema you see only one film. We used to see two and the Pathé News. At the end they would play *God Save The Queen* and everybody would stand to attention. That's if you were not quick enough to leave when the film finished. On Sunday nights we would go to the Capitol Cinema to see and hear live bands. We paid 2s 6d or 3s. You had to climb up about forty steps in the Empire. Up in the Gods we called it. And they were wooden seats!

Joan Burnell

Hippodrome and Central

When you paid your tuppence entrance to the Hippodrome in Westgate Street you were handed a steel token about four inches by two inches. You then climbed a winding stone stairway which was quite a journey to the top of the stairs, where you gave your token to the commissionaire. If the cinema was full you could always find a seat behind a steel support which meant you could only see half the screen by ducking to the left or right. The Central Cinema in The Hayes was the cheapest cinema in Cardiff and no matter where you sat you always had a good view. The staff

Interior of the Capitol Cinema which closed in 1978.

THE PROPRIETORS & MANAGEMENT OF THIS THEATRE
ARE OPPOSED TO SUNDAY OPENING AND INVITE
ITS PATRONS TO VOTE AGAINST.

The Central Cinema which closed in 1958.

were very friendly and most of the patrons were from the docks area.

Charles Harlin

Warwick Hall

When I was in my teens there was a dance hall at the back of Whitchurch Road called the Warwick Hall. I had to be in at 10 o'clock at night or else. I remember running down Albany Road and looking at the post office clock and I was eighteen then! I had a wind-up gramophone which was given to me by my next door neighbour with some records. One was called *Oh, For The Wings Of A Dove* and another *Casey At The Dentist*. We used to buy records in Woolworths for sixpence. I remember our radio too. We had what they called a Cat's Whisker. It had a pair of earphones and, if you put them in a large basin on the table, we could all hear it otherwise it was only the person with the earphones that could hear it.

Gaynor Rosser

The Iron Horse

I regularly visited Roath Park with my husband, my two sons and my daughter. The children would ride the iron horse and my daughter was always fascinated by a hole in the ground as the water from the lake would lap in and out. We even used to walk to Roath Park when we moved to Llanishen in 1955. When my children grew up we used to take their children to feed the ducks and play in the park.

Mrs J. Francis

The iron horse, Roath Park, c. 1950.

The Francis family feeding the swans in Roath Park, c. 1950.

Onward Christian Soldiers

We used to go to dances in St Cyprian's Hall and then they had a dramatic society which I joined. We used to have the Whitsun Treats at the top of Penylan Hill. There were all fields there then. At St Cyprian's we had to form a prossession with banners and walk to Mackintosh Place singing *Onward Christian Soldiers*.

Gladys Jenkins

Open Air Baths

When I was a young girl my father and mother would often take my twin brothers and myself to Llandaff Fields, where we

Mrs Gladys Jenkins, 1999.

learned to swim in the open-air baths. I can remember a pavilion with a stage and we used to watch dancing troupes and male and female comics performing on the stage. We used to enjoy these outings very much. During the war years the fields area was dug up and vegetables were grown there at allotments to help towards the war effort.

Margaret L. Jones

Caravan Holidays

My uncle, Bill Stamp, had a caravan and in the early 1950s he would take me, my mother and father, cousin Gill and her mother, my aunt Minnie, on holiday. How the six of us all managed to sleep in that little caravan I will never know. One year we went to Blackpool and we saw the film star Errol Flynn. My aunt got him to autograph a ten shilling note, but I don't know what become of it.

Jacqueline Lee

Walking and Courting

In those days when we were courting we did an awful lot of walking. All the housing estates today like Llanrumney, Gabalfa and Ely were all open fields.

Stan Sorenson

The Bryants and Stamps caravan holiday, c. 1951.

The Carlton, Queen Street, c. 1920.

Tuppenny Bloods

There wasn't any radio or television in those days so the main indoor activity was reading and, apart from library books, there were the great tuppenny bloods such as the Wizard, Hotspur, Rover, Adventure and Bulls Eye. Each seemed to come out on a different day. We couldn't afford more than one or two, but swapping more or less ensured we read all we fancied. Many cigarette manufacturers issued picture cards in their packets. These usually comprised of fifty or fifty-two a set. No empty packet lying in the street went unchecked. The object was to collect a full set and this was usually achieved by swapping. Surplus cards were used for playing pitch and toss. Wills brought out a set which depicted famous paintings and two I remember were Mother and Son and Boyhood of Raleigh. The fifty cards were like a jigsaw puzzle and when you had the set you sent them to Wills and received a proper picture in return. Other popular series were footballers, cricketers, motor vehicles, battleships and all manner of sea going craft.

Jos Dwyer

Hall Of Glamour

I used to love going to the City Hall dances. You had to queue right across the road. We used to call it the Hall of Glamour.

Mary Jackson

The Carlton

The Carlton in Queen Street used to be very popular as a meeting place. We used to

The civic centre, c. 1950.

drink Russian tea in very tall glasses. No milk, just a slice of lemon. The pastries there were delicious.

Ruth Hobbs

Dancing Shoes

In the 1930s, I paid 5s for my first pair of dancing shoes. I first learnt to dance at the Regent Dance Hall in Mardy Street, Grangetown and admission was 9d.

Mrs R. Richards

Swimming

Swimming was a great pastime in those days of my youth. You had the Guildford Crescent, Llandaff and the Splott Baths.

And during the summer months there was nothing better than to have a free dip in the sea at Penarth, Lavernock or Barry Island. If we were short of money for the train fare it wouldn't take too long to carry a few cases of luggage for people coming off the train at Queen's Street railway station and picking up a few bob and pooling it between us.

Ron Davies

Singing Cowboys

The films I liked were musicals. I wasn't struck on anything else, but I liked the musical cowboy films. People like Gene Autry and Roy Rogers.

John Attree

Tea and Buns

There were loads of dance halls then and the one I started off in was the Regent in Grangetown. I learned to dance there. There was no drink in the dance halls then just tea and buns.

Philip Donovan

Billy The Seal

I was born in the west side of the city of Cardiff in 1924 at No. 40 Fairfield Avenue, so called because there were fields at the end of our street when the houses only went up to No. 56. We were very near to Victoria Park which at that time had some pretty flower beds, a large circular grass playground,

Splott open air swimming baths, c. 1960.

Left: *A rare picture of the legendary Billy the Seal.* Right: *The October floods in Fairfield Avenue, Victoria Park, in 1927.*

and a small zoo which consisted of a monkey house, several cages of guinea pigs, a wallaby and tortoises. I walked through the park practically nearly every day with my best friend to both the infant and elementary schools sometimes lingering on the way to watch and call to the famous Billy the Seal.

If we carried a shopping bag with us while walking through the park, Billy would swim rapidly from one end of the pond to the other following us along hoping for a meal. When we did feed Billy we would call out 'Over Billy' and she would turn over two or three times before taking the fish. She escaped during the flood caused by the overflowing of the Ely River in 1927 and swam down what is now Cowbridge Road

East. She lived to a good old age and we missed her when she died in 1939.

Ruby Howe

The Bug House

The Coronet Cinema in Woodville Road was the nearest fleapit or local cinema to where I lived. Sadly, it was knocked down to make way for a petrol station, but is now a block of flats. It was at the Cora, or Bug House, as we usually called it, that I went to see the film *Buffalo Bill* in the 1940s. In those days we kids played Cowboys and Indians. Little did I realize it then that Buffalo Bill had ridden along Woodville Road, raising his hat to all and sundry as he led a big parade, on his first visit to Cardiff back in 1891. The Globe, which used to be in Albany Road, was another fleapit that wasn't far from where I lived. It was the first cinema where I ever sat in the upstairs posh seats. On this particular night my mother my Aunt Sarah and my sister Valerie and me had queued for so long in the rain to see *Random Harvest*, starring Greer Garson and Ronald Colman, that the manager took pity on us and escorted us to the expensive upstairs seats. Fifty years ago these local little cinemas played a big part in our lives. Now they are just memories.

Brian Lee

Central Cinema

The best cinema then was the Central. It was only 2d or 4d. If there was an 'A' certificate film showing you had to have an adult to accompany you. So as young boys we would ask someone to take us in. Things were a lot safer in those days. We all liked the Central because you had two good pictures, a newsreel and a comedy short. And the programme changed twice a week.

Philip Donovan

The Globe Cinema closed in 1985.

The Plaza

The Plaza Cinema was a regular haunt of mine. The films used to be changed twice a week. I remember the queue used to wind down North Road into Longspeare Avenue when there was a popular film showing. The Saturday morning shows were great fun. How we used to cheer for Roy Rogers and his horse Trigger. Flash Gordon was another favourite. We would boo all the baddies and the place would be in an uproar.

Diana Prichard

Billy Brian Junior with the Lee Cup awarded to his father in 1904.

My First Concert

My very first concert was at the City Lodge later known as St David's Hospital. I played and sang *When the Angels Played Their Harps For Me*. The Cathays Male Voice Choir was also there and they made me, more or less, their number one draw. I also sang in the Seamen's Mission down the docks together with my uncle Jim Champion who was a comedian. Later I joined St Andrews Amateur Operatic Society in their production of *Dorothy*.

Evelyn Pincott

The Splott Cinema

I can recall the Splott Cinema when they had silent films. A tall, thin man played the piano and a lady played the violin. The Splott Cinema was the mecca for all children on a Saturday afternoon. One of the films was the *Green Archer* and strangely enough the film did have a green tint to it. Later when the silent films finished the first talkie in the Splott Cinema was called *Rio Rita*. The Splott, like all cinemas then, was luxurious. They were picture palaces as the name suggested done out in this art decor style.

Edward J. Kendrick

Trick Cyclist

My father, Bill Brian, was a trick cyclist who won numerous awards for his daredevil feats. In 1904 he cycled from Newport to Cardiff

Billy Brian performing one of his bicycle balancing acts, c. 1905.

WANTED

RICO BANDELLO

'DUKE' MANTEE

TOM POWERS

THE DOSSIER ON THESE PUBLIC ENEMIES AND OTHER MEMBERS OF THE 'WARNER BROTHERS GANG' IS BEING EXPOSED BY:

THE CANTON FILM APPRECIATION GROUP

COMMENCING ON MARCH 12th 1971

LIMITED MEMBERSHIP

GENTLEMEN ONLY

MEETINGS EVERY ALTERNATE FRIDAY

For full details write to:

*The Canton Film Appreciation Group
235, Cowbridge Road East,
Canton, Cardiff.*

● MEMBER OF THE BRITISH FEDERATION OF FILM SOCIETIES

The Canton Film Appreciation Group poster, 1971.

backwards without stopping and was presented with the Lee Cup. I recall him telling me that in 1906 the famed music hall comedian Dan Leno presented him with a prize at a show in Sophia Gardens for staging the most entertaining event.

He did all kinds of balancing acts on his bicycle riding backwards around Roath Park Lake and up Leckwith Hill and Thorn Hill. No matter how bad the weather he cycled through the streets to do his shopping with his umbrella open. One year the great German trick cyclist Bud Snyder was appearing at the Empire Theatre. He begged my father to join him in his act, but Dad turned him down and stayed with Spillers and Bakers where he worked as a clerk for forty years. He was only 5ft tall and made eight attempts to join the army when the First World War broke out. But they turned him down on each occasion as he had heart trouble. When he married at the age of twenty-nine he was given only a few years to live. Although small in stature, he was a strong and determined man and the fact that he lived a further forty years is surely proof of his determination to prove the doctors wrong.

Bill Brian Jnr

Canton Film Group

In 1961 I started the Canton Film Appreciation Group which became a little bit famous shall we say. It was a small, very special group, but we did quite a lot of interesting things. We had official seasons where actors or directors would nominate their favourite films. The first official season was Laurel and Hardy and Stan

Letter from Edward G. Robinson.

Laurel did a recorded tape for us. Our honorary associates included: Edgar G. Robinson, Richard Attenborough, Fritz Lang, Laurence Olivier and Michael Bolton.

Dennis Pope

Tram Rides

The Cardiff tram lines ended at Victoria Park. For the sum of two pence halfpenny we would take a round trip to Roath Park and back. That was money in those days. The never ceasing excitement of their clang and clatter, their unreliable overhead

Trams came to Cardiff in 1902.

electric arm which so often overran the rails were a never ending joy. The driver and conductor would be obliged to leave the tram and reverse the overhead rails for the return journey. The ribald remarks from passengers on the top deck failed to disturb their solid serenity. We kids adored them. To us they were the knights of the road.

Phyllis Anderson

Chattering Monkeys

In Victoria Park we saw chattering monkeys, unconversational parrots, an inscrutable eagle, a restless fox and everybody's friend Billy the Seal floundering in his pond.

Margaret Williams

Beautiful Flowers

My great delight was when Dad drove us to see Billy the Seal at Victoria Park. She was quite wonderful with her tricks and her loving manner. Even in those days we as a family loved the beautiful flowers and greenery of Victoria Park.

Betty McLeod

Street Games

One popular street game that was played in the Canton area before the First World War was as follows: About ten or twelve children would line up, with arms linked, in two rows of six aside, at a distance of some twelve to fifteen feet apart. One side would walk forward whilst chanting the following lines: 'Are you ready to fight? Ee... Ii... Ober... Are you ready to fight? For we're Roman soldiers.' The other side would then advance chanting their reply: 'Yes, we're ready for a fight for we're British soldiers.' No fight took place, however, only lots of shouts and laughter. I have often wondered whether this game was, in fact, handed down from ancient times, from one generation of children to the next. Perhaps the reason for its demise was the growing popularity of the motorcar.

Skipping too was popular either on one's own, or over a rope held by two other children. Another game was hopscotch over the pavement slabs which were numbered with pieces of chalk. Then there was whip and top which usually commenced at the same time in succeeding years, usually in the spring.

Ruth Hobbs

Mari Lwyd

There was a Christmas custom to visit public houses with a Mari Lwyd (which was a model of a horse's head worn over the shoulders with a workable mouth). The person wearing the horse's head would enter the pub and sing a carol. If he wasn't given a drink or some money he would then playfully bite the ones who didn't respond. On New Year's Eve folk would stand at their front doors and see the New Year in. On Halloween, which we called Ducking Apple Day, a large tin bath would be filled with water then some apples would be put in it. The game was to eat the apples while they were floating. Another custom was to wait on a stone stile, of which there were many in Whitchurch, to see the devil appear. I never saw him once although I waited. Yet another custom was to lay hay and straw on the road outside the house of a

The monkey house, Victoria Park, c. 1919.

The Mari Lwyd was an old Christmas time custom throughout Wales.

seriously ill person to deaden the sounds of horses' hooves and cart wheels.

Thomas E. Broad

would trip over the mats to everyone's amusement.

Jos Dwyer

Rat, Tap Ginger

A rather nasty game became fashionable at one time called Rat, Tap Ginger. An unpleasant adult was sorted out, and doormats, collected from the porches of other houses, were piled against his door. A piece of string would be attached to his door knocker and from across the road his door was knocked. When he opened it he would be met with a barrage of uncomplimentary remarks. Then when he rushed out to chase us in the dark he

Seaside Trips

In the years between the wars, a favourite treat was a trip to the seaside at Penarth, Lavernock, St Mary's Bay, Swanbridge, Sully or Barry Island. The rail fare from Grangetown station to Penarth, for example was 3d return – about 1p in our present coinage – and other destinations only slightly more. Another popular venue for a family picnic was the Subway. This was the tongue at the mouth of the River Ely, beyond the Windsor Slipway, where the foot tunnel under the River Ely came to the surface. The toll through the Subway, when the turnstile was manned, was a penny and it was the quickest and easiest route for men working at Penarth Dock.

Families would come and picnic on the rough turf and scrub that surrounded the red-brick building, play baseball, or go beach combing along the foreshore. We would take the household iron kettle, beg some water from the Subway attendant, then boil it over a plumber's blow lamp to make tea. This, with bread and jam sandwiches on a fine summer's afternoon, was high living.

Other half-day adventure walks were made to the Droves, the woods of Llandough, Leckwith and Cwrt-yr-Ala Park, always keeping a careful lookout for gamekeepers and wardens who would send you packing with a clip around the ear if they caught you. There is the story of the gamekeeper with an impediment in his

The building of the Leckwith Bridge before the last war.

The old Glamorgan Canal, North Road, c. 1930.

speech who caught a young lad in the woods picking primroses. The young lad, by coincidence also had an impediment in his speech – a cleft palate – and when he answered the gamekeeper's questions got a severe belt around the ear for making fun!

The old Leckwith Hill was a narrow, steep winding downhill race to the sharp turn over the river bridge at the bottom and some years before the Second World War, I saw a new bridge opened by Sir Leslie Hore-Belisha, the Minister of Transport and inventor of the Belisha Crossing. Penarth Road toll gate was still in private hands and the new road enabled a lot of traffic to be cheaply diverted around it to Penarth and Barry.

Stanley J. Adams

The Tidefields

The Tidefields and Splott Park had a particular attraction especially when the spring tides came up. People used to walk along the sea wall and men raced whippets there. In those days there were also air circuses brought there by Sir Alan Cobham. That would be around 1930. There was wing walking and delayed parachute jumping attempts on the world record. I well remember a little airplane called the *Flying Flea*. There was wonderful entertainment for everybody. Air trips cost five shillings but most people never had the money to afford them.

Edward J. Kendrick

Street Games

Day and weekend life outside school revolved around play. The streets were filled with children playing group games. The boys were obsessed with football and I frequently took part in street matches, using a tennis ball, which ended with the score at something like '40-38 disputed' and only terminated after dark when our mothers called us in for supper. Our wise and prudent mothers made sure that we used only our oldest shoes! Our long-suffering neighbours would eventually move us on and we would quite happily move to the next street corner and continue. When the ball went into a garden it was necessary for the kicker to climb in to retrieve the ball. Most householders were very reasonable about this, I now realize, and I recall one who would patiently explain how to kick with knee over ball to keep the ball from rising. We constantly played with marbles or alleys, as we called them, either on chalked targets or along the gutters in the streets. When an alley went down a drain, we pulled open the grating and felt for the missing item in the sink!

There were other boys' games such as Bomberino, a very physical game, and we were not above joining; the girls to play Bad Eggs, Mob, Hopscotch and skipping games. Apart from the streets there were few places in which to play. The Army Barracks field was of course out of bounds although we did occasionally venture in. The Maindy Pool had been filled in between the wars, and after World War Two was converted into a sports stadium. During the war it was used for storage by the council, and to the fury of the caretaker, who limped, we used to run across the tops of the tar barrels and jump into the sand piles.

The banks of the quarry sides were overgrown with superb wild blackberry bushes from which we used to pick the berries. Across the other side of North Road the old Glamorgan Canal was still in existence although unused. There were at some spots the decaying remains of barges,

and at Kingsway little boys dived into the canal feeder for thrown coins. The Castle grounds were still owned by the Marquis of Bute and therefore rarely open to the public.

Behind Maindy Road was an open area, between the lane behind the houses and the railway, known as the Brickies. It was here that the briquettes used by the vessels of Scott of the Antarctic for fuel had been made. I tried my first cigarette at the Brickies – a Spanish one which we all shared and which made me feel ill. I never smoked again. I also had a fight with John Biddlecome which I won: memorable because I almost never got involved in a fight, particularly in the school playground.

Then as now, Roath Park Lake was a mecca for Cardiffians and throughout my young days I frequently walked around the lake. One day John Burgess and I went their by ourselves and unfortunately fell in. We arrived home as dusk fell, to be greeted by anxious and annoyed parents and neighbours.

Geoff Bray

Dancing Group

I did belong to a little dancing group it was in Clive Road. My cousin and I were about the same age when we learned to dance and we were taken there by our mothers. We had to go in this big house in Clive Road and climb the stairs to the attic. But we enjoyed ourselves and did a bit of everything – acrobatics, ballet dancing and singing at St Luke's when they had a church bazaar.

Ruby Howe

Clive Road children's dancing group, c. 1929.

Sunday Concerts

Public entertainment was mainly the cinema, the theatre, variety and orchestral concerts – but only on weekdays. Sunday was the Sabbath day to be kept in sterile holiness and everything shut down except the churches and chapels. What a breakthrough it was when Waldini was allowed to hold concerts of popular music, not too popular, on Sunday evenings at 8 p.m. so people could go to church first. Two of his leading performers were Elaine, the shy girl on the accordion, and the one-legged drummer, who sang when required. The expression vocalist was unknown and he was a singer who didn't need a microphone to be heard all over the hall.

The Post Office Band used to hold a public concert in the Capitol or Empire Theatre on Good Friday evenings. These concerts were usually well patronized even if only because there was no other counter attraction on the day, but as a playing member, I like to think that our music ability helped to draw the audience. Long before the event, the programme had to be submitted for approval to the Watch Committee of the City Council, dominated by the dour, unyielding champion of non-conformist morality, the Revd Penry Thomas. The programme was chosen in the knowledge that it would have to get the Watch Committee's consent. Imagine our dismay and bewilderment one year when they rejected the classical overture *Zampa* as being unsuitable.

Stanley J. Adams

The Embassy Skating Rink

I remember the Embassy Skating Rink re-opening in March 1951. It was bought by Thomson and Baker of Rotherham. Mr and Mrs Dennis and Marion Bate were brought in to manage it. The skating club was started soon after it's opening. One of the first chairmen was Jack Smith the local butcher in Cathays Terrace. Marion Bate

managed the café and she was helped by Betty Kane. Betty lived in Gabalfa and both her children skated also. George Morgan who lived in Australia Road became the honorary district rep for Wales. Haydn Davies and David Parry, who both lived in Roath, went on to play for England. In 1959 I married Haydn and he still teaches the youngsters in Barry. I became professional roller dance champion in 1956 and my partner was Ted Norton. I also became the first lady to win the first class medal for teaching and knowledge of the sport and I am still the only lady to do so today. Only two other people attained that credit. The skating surface was well known for its peculiar shape, almost wedge shaped, but the surface of maple was superb to skate on. The

Waldini's Gipsy Band was popular in Cardiff in the 1930s.

Roller dance skating champions Shielah Bates and Ted Norton, 1956.

Some of the original members of the Embassy roller skating rink, c. 1952.

Welsh National Championship soon became a major event and was well supported by skaters from all over. The rink also had great fancy dress events and parties for children. Saturday mornings and afternoons were very popular and there were always queues up the street waiting for it to open.

Sheilah Davies

The Barry Island Train

Children jumping up and down excited,
Porters shouting 'Mind your backs'.
Pigeons cooing in their baskets,
Mam gives Billy several smacks.

'He's got Five Boys Chocolate on his trousers.'
Dulcie smirks behind her hand.
Sunshine beams through station rafters,
Enhancing magic wonderland.

'Mam!, can I go to the lav?' I ask.
'Trust you to be awkward' in her resigned voice.
'Billy take your brother's hand,'
Grudgingly; he has no choice.

Hooray!, here she comes, dead on time.
She halts, seething and fuming,
Indignation,
The footbridge vanishes in a cloud of steam,
At the Cardiff General Station.

The driver, peak capped and dungareed,
Wipes his hand on cotton waste.
The fireman consumes cold tea,
And sandwiches of salmon paste.

Cardboard boxes full of chicks,
Bikes and pigeons, bags of mail,
Fill the guards van's ample space,
In transit, courtesy Great Western Rail.

We occupy the corner seats,
The Ashton's Poultry bag on Mama's lap,
Contains our bathers, bottled pop,
And Dulcie's bathing cap.

We stand respectfully, for the fat lady.
Who, undoes her blouse with podgy hand.
And, quite naturally,
feeds the smallest of her band.

'Dulcie, stop your fidgeting.'
'It's my knickers Mam.
The 'lastics broke, its too thin.'
'Well, come here, and turn around,
I'll fix them with a safety pin.'

The lady with the rimless glasses,
Views the scene with some askance.
Then resumes with contemplation,
The sepia pictures of Penzance.

Her pigtailed charges sit besides her.
Billy, who doesn't give a fig,
Pokes his tongue out.
The elder sister, mouths quite clearly,
'You horrid little pig.'

A man with moustache and bowler hat,
Boards the train, gasping and pale.
With attaché case upon the rack,
He unfolds his Western Mail!

The guard, who after all, is in charge,
Whistles to proceed.
The engine gives a joyous whoop,
And slowly gathers speed.

'Goodbye!' We wave, our joy complete.
The clickety-clack of each rail joint,
A dialogue to childish ears,
Jacksons Bay, Whitmore and Nells Point.

A whole long year we've waited,
For this journey to the sea.
We won't forget you God for this.
Mam, Dulcie, Billy and me.

Edward J. Kendrick

for a ready made swing. We had endless
games of football of course, kick the tin,
whip and top, strong horses and baseball. It
was recognized in the playing of these games
it was 'pay for your own china'. This meant
that if you did any damage to a window and
so on you or your parents paid.

Jim Cowley

Street was Playground

The street was also our playground in the
days when cars were few and far between.
The lamp-posts served as a ready made
wicket for our cricket matches and the girls
used the lamp-post arms hung up with ropes

*Valerie Lee and her brother
Brian. Barry Island sands,
c. 1938.*

CHAPTER 5

Wartime

Wounded soldiers being taken to Albany Road school during the first war.

Hospital Schools

During the First World War some schools were converted into hospitals. And when the ambulance trains arrived at Cardiff Central station a silent crowd would gather outside to watch as the wounded heroes were carried on stretchers into the waiting motor ambulances. People visited the hospitals and adopted Tommies whose families lived in distant parts of the country. We had one patient one year, a Mr Young, and my mother took him cakes and things just as though he was related to one of the family. To while away the time when convalescing many soldiers did embroidery and pen painting on black satin. This pen painting involved a printed design, sprinkled with a special kind of what I would call sand.

Soldiers collected silk pictures from cigarette packets and appliquéd them on material to make cushions which no doubt became gifts for their nearest and dearest.

Margaret Williams

Bombed houses in St Agnes Road, Heath, 1943.

Bombed Out

I was born in Manor Street, Heath, and I had two brothers named Jack and Robert and a sister Gillian. After living at Manor Street for a while we moved to 84 Coburn Street at my Aunty Gert's house. Later we moved to No. 36 where we were bombed during the blitz. Because we had no place to live, we went to my Nana Roberts house at 11 Allensbank Road. Going back to the night we were bombed, that's a night I will never forget. The house just collapsed around us and we had to climb over the rubble to get out. When the bomb dropped I was under the kitchen table and my mother and baby brother Robert were in the pantry because we didn't have an air-raid shelter. A bomb fell three doors away in the Davies's house when little Margaret was killed and her brother Edgar. We also got bombed in Allensbank Road. A landmine fell in the cemetery so again we all had to move out while the house got repaired.

Joan Burnell

Air Raids

I was fifteen years of age when the Second World War broke out. At the time I was on holiday with my parents and younger sisters staying with my widowed grandmother. After our holiday we returned to Cardiff and I continued at Cathays High School until I was eighteen. There were many air-raids on Cardiff during that period. We originally did not have an air-raid shelter, but shared a neighbour's. To do this we had to get over a garden wall and my father built a step our side to make it easier to get over. Whenever the air-raid warning went we took shelter and later when the air-raids became more frequent we had our own air-raid shelter.

There were seats on either side, not much room I recall, but we had torches and plenty of blankets. Later my grandmother gave up her home and came to stay with us so we had to help her down the shelter. My father was a member of the Cardiff City Police and he always had to report for duty when the air-raid warning went off. Mother was also an authorized collector for the Red Cross Fund 'Penny A Week' Appeal and went to every house in the street to collect the pennies.

Reta Gale

Over Paid, Over Sexed and Over Here

I remember the Yanks in a field not 100 yards from our house. They had chocolate and chewing gum and were generous with their rations of corned beef, ham, and Camel and Lucky Strike cigarettes. 'Hey Kid, got any big sisters?' We always said 'yes'

because they would give us more. They gave the girls nylons and took them off again. Ha Ha!

Alan T. Grainger

Tomatoes and Sugar

My father invited two US officers home one memorable evening. They were charming brought presents including comics and gum for me, and I was intrigued to see them eat tomatoes with sugar.

Geoff Bray

Earliest Memory

My earliest memory is of the Second World War and mother wrapping me up in a blanket and carrying me downstairs to the Anderson air raid shelter at the bottom of our garden in Thesiger Street. A year or two later I was big enough for my uncle, Philip Donovan, to cart me around in the carrier of his bicycle to see the bomb damaged streets. I distinctly remember him cycling over Woodville Road Bridge and I only have to pass the spot today for the memory to come flooding back.

Brian Lee

Searchlights

I can remember the preparations for the attacks which would come from the air.

Llandaff Cathedral, which was damaged by bombing during the Second World War.

Barrage balloons floated above the city, in order to deter low flying planes. An air raid shelter was built in our garden, and in most other gardens. Exposed windows were criss-crossed with sticky tape. Railings were taken to be used in the war effort, except those surrounding the grass areas in the centre of Gelligaer and Rhigos Gardens, which were converted into allotments for growing fruit and vegetables. Street lights were extinguished, and car headlamps were covered except for a small slit. And ration books with coupons to limit consumption of essential food and sweets, became very important in our daily lives. Dad joined the Home Guard and although this didn't have much impact on my personal life I do remember them practising with stirrup pumps and buckets of water and sand. When the air raids began in mid-1940, the sound of the warning sirens followed a quick trip down the garden path to the shelter became a regular nightly occurrence. I suggested that the others should go but that I would like to stay in bed, but this was not favourably received. We had a box from which to step down into the underground shelter and conditions were at first a bit primitive in the shelter. However, one night a bomb went off fairly nearby just as Dad was carrying my sister Margaret down the path and he fell in the shelter hurriedly. Proper steps and bunk beds were soon introduced!

Sounds are often move evocative than other memory stirrers. I can, with others of my generation, still easily recall the warning siren, the drone of bombers and the higher sound of fighter plane engines, the crumping sound of anti-aircraft guns, the whistle of falling bombs, and the different wavering sound of the all-clear siren. The sight of searchlights sweeping the skies was impressive. It was generally said that the bombers were more likely to come on a clear moonlit night, and this was certainly the case on 2 January 1941 when Cardiff suffered its worse raid. The raid lasted all night, and resulted in over 150 deaths.

Canton High School and Llandaff Cathedral were hit on that night: considering how close Cathays is to the centre, we were lucky. However, Dad was fire watching on the roof of Cross Brothers and saw the intensity of the bombing at close quarters. In Cardiff everybody was issued with gas masks, to be carried at all times in cardboard containers, although women often replaced their containers with more elegant carriers.

Geoff Bray

No Butter

I always remember the day war broke out. My mother was terribly upset. I can remember her saying 'Now you will know there's a war on. You will have to eat margarine instead of butter.'

Ruby Howe

Top To Toe

As a child in Ordell Street in Splott we didn't have a bathroom or even hot water. But every night we were washed from top to toe in a bowl. One night we were halfway through this ritual when the sirens went. I remember my mother peeping around the back door to check the sky then saying run! We all ran down the garden to the

Ruby Howe gives her father and brother a helping hand with the air raid shelter.

Anderson shelter my brother carrying the baby, another brother carrying soap and towel and my mother bringing up the rear with the bowl. Not even Hitler's bombers could stop us finishing our nightly scrub.

Valerie Snell

Voluntary Work

During the war years my father was involved with the Royal Observer Corps and he used to go on duty every week at a mansion in Insole Court, Llandaff. I also used to do some voluntary work there. Everything was hush-hush at the time as they used to track down the enemy aircraft coming over the country. I remember my parents used to invite wounded soldiers, recovering in Rookwood Hospital, for afternoon tea on Sundays. We were always baking cakes, as best we could, the day before they came.

Margaret L. Jones

Stark Naked

I was called up for a medical in St John's School by The Friary. I still had the dressings on from my burst appendicitis operation. I had to strip off stark naked. There were four doctors I think doing different parts of you. The first chap that looked at me called the other three over and said 'Have a look at this'. They decided I was grade 4 and didn't bother me any more.

John Attree

Covered In Dust

Our house and home was covered in dust. My mother muttering, 'Dear God, Oh God help us'. There was a hole in the ceiling, right through the roof, you could see the sky. An incendiary bomb had burnt its way right through. The local fire watch had contained the fire, but what a mess. We all pitched in together and cleaned as best we could. Barrage balloon material for the roof and within days we had settled back in the old routine. Myself collecting coal from the foreshore and timber from the dock. Had to keep the home fire burning.

Alan T. Grainger

Cupboard under the Stairs

My main wartime memories are of running home from St Joseph's School in Whitchurch Road when the air raid warning went off. And as my mother was sure that we children would catch pneumonia in our garden shelter, we always went in the cupboard under the stairs during raids. We were there, even for the worst raid of all on 1 January 1941 when my brother aged sixteen was terminally ill at home. He died on 5 January. My mother's theory was that the staircase remained even in a bombed house unless it had a direct hit. I also recall tombstones going through the roofs of the houses in Gelligaer Street, the Whitchurch Road end, when landmines were dropped all around us. The Germans were aiming for the railway lines north and south of Gelligaer Street and nearby Maindy Barracks no doubt. We would have great fun, however, the day following air raids when we would collect shrapnel on our way to school. I also remember being very proud of the fact that my dad was Gelligaer Street's chief fire watcher and the street stirrup-pump was kept at our house. We had a sign outside which stated ' Stirrip Pump Kept Here'

Monica Walsh

Deep Snow

It was in 1943 that we had the heavy snow and it was thanks to the Americans stationed over here that we had any clearance of the roads. They had all the heavy equipment and that sort of thing. The snow was very deep. Everything came to a standstill, absolutely everything.

John Attree

Landmines On Llandaff

We were in direct line of the landmines that fell on Landaff Cathedral and St Michael's College. We were under the stairs my mother, my father and myself my brother being in the forces. Oh, the blast was terrible, I have never known anything like it. It ripped right down the side of the house and we thought the side of the house was gone. I remember my father's astonishment when he came back and told us the wall was still standing. After the war the whole side of the house was taken down and rebuilt. We had a Morrison air raid shelter, which was like a great big metal table with mesh around it and it was in the breakfast room. For months I slept on a camp bed under the stairs, as it was the safest place to be. I can remember that Morrison table because it had vicious

corners on it and if you hit it you had lovely big bruises on your thighs.

Mrs John

Avenue of Trees

During the last war, the 2nd Evacuation Unit of the United States Army was encamped on Whitchurch Common. Before they left for the invasion, they planted an avenue of trees on the common to thank the people of Whitchurch for their hospitality. A plaque which read 'This Avenue Of Trees Was Planted On Behalf of the 2nd Evacuation Unit of the United States Army As A Token of Gratitude For The Hospitality Extended To Them By The Parishioners Of Whitchurch

John and Vera Attree (first and second left) with neighbours during the deep snow of 1943.

St. David's Day Essay, 1940.

How the war has affected the City of Cardiff.

The chief effect of the war on our city is created by the black-out. On account of it, the time of the afternoon session at elementary schools was altered. By this new arrangement the children were able to get home in the daylight. The new rule operated from November until January, when evenings are longer than usual. The shops now close earlier but soon they will be reverting to the former hours. The transport services have also been re-arranged. The road toll has greatly increased and quite a number of accidents are caused by pedestrian unthinkingly flashing their torches in an upward direction, thus temporarily blinding motorists. With torches becoming almost a necessity, there was a rush on batteries and a shortage has resulted.

Through war risk insurance, among other causes, the price of food has risen considerably. The snag here is that most employers do not pay war bonuses to their employees as they did in the Great War, and, generally speaking, the increased cost of living is a strain on the pocket of the average working man. Rationing, so far, has not seriously affected anyone, the only difficulty being the small portion of butter allowed to each individual. Most people finish their ration before the end of the week and margarine has to be used. However, this is only a minor detail and nearly everyone agrees that the best quality margarine is superior to the butter we've been getting recently.

Barrage balloons can be seen over the vital spots of the city, and occasionall the anti-aircraft batteries in different neighbourhoods use their searchlights to scan the skies for imaginary raiders. Apart from this, and the few facts already mentioned, life in Cardiff is quite normal.

By Peter Walsh.

An essay written and typed by Peter Walsh who sadly died in 1941.

Peter Walsh seated far right at a Coronation Street party, 1936.

106

During The Second World War 1939-1945', was placed each end to commemorate the occasion.

Eirfryn Lowe

Evacuation

For me, an even greater terror than the air raids was the trauma of evacuation. From the only world we knew – Splott – we were herded together, labelled, names etc. tied with string, carrying our meagre belongings and gas masks. We were bundled, just like our belongings, on to the train amidst cries of 'Stay together, stay together.' Children, inconsolable, mothers crying, kisses, hugs, but firm farewells. Where were we going? – Maerdy. To a boy from Splott it was the other side of the moon. Even now,

more than fifty years on, I remember as a child, in the early hours of the morning, suddenly and abruptly being rudely awakened from the innocence of sleep that only a child can know. Dragged from that warmth and security, lifted up and out into the cold night air, my Dad running down the street clutching me to his chest, dashing through a swirl of people against the flow of their panic. A cacophony of noise, bright glowing lights, the customary blackout now a dazzling display of vivid lights. My father's heart pounding in unison with mine, as he ran, carrying me to a neighbour's air raid shelter. The echoing Boom, Boom, of the Ack, Ack guns in a nearby field exploding in our defence, injected bolts of adrenaline into the chambers of our hearts. The drone of distant aircraft, the ghost like apparitions of lit-up barrage balloons hovering overhead and the unreal reality of it all. My dad's breath labouring upon my face,

The United States Army plaque.

Clifton Street Police Station in the 1930s.

his countenance a mixture of anxiety and excitement. Tumbling through a terraced house, into the garden, down the steps and our goal is reached. I am handed to the secure and comforting arms of my mother. The small womb-like cramped shelter, already overcrowded with the occupancy of three adults and six children, the smell of paraffin from the single lamp, the tiny glow of candle from within the usual jam jar cast flickering shadows upon the corrugated sheeting of the shelter. My mother's comforting voice and care worn face soothed and calmed my unease. Why did we all whisper quietly to each other? Perhaps we thought the Germans might hear us!

A billy-can of hot, sweet tea, nervous conversation, a child crying fitfully. The Boom, Boom of explosion vibrating through our shelter. Suddenly, once again, we are roused into reality. The clatter of boots from above and the rusty bolt is dragged free. A gush of cold but fresh air bursts in upon us. Boots appear and at first view hearts stop. Could it be the Germans? Then the reassuring sound of Dad's voice talking to his mate, their deep laughter, blackened faces and bright eyes flush with excitement – they had been on picket duty – come into view. We are safe. Laughter and tears and more tea, some sandwiches, some sleep, some life.

A.T. Grainger

Field Marshal Montgomery

One of my few precious possessions is a letter I had from Field Marshal Bernard Montgomery. I had it framed and it reads: 'I feel I cannot let you return to civil life without a message of thanks and farewell. Together we have carried through one of the most successful campaigns in history, and it has been our good fortune to be members of a great team. God Bless and God Speed, B.L. Montgomery, Field Marshal, Commander in Chief, BOAR 1945.'

Bill Brian, Junior

Cardiff's Heaviest Bombing

I think it was in 1941, the night of Cardiff's heaviest bombing. I was working in a government department at the time and the office was in Cowbridge Road, near Rawden Place. We were working late and it was quite dark, when suddenly it became quite light outside. Rushing to the window we saw hundreds of flares coming down which we stared at fascinated. Then the first bomb fell and we were ordered down to the air raid shelter. My husband, Lyn Josty, who was stationed at Ferry Road prior to going overseas in the army, came to meet me from the office and he joined us in the air raid shelter. Bombs fell at a distance for some time, then one terrific crash which sounded next door. It was a frightful sound and we were all shaken. When in the small hours we walked home through broken glass and rubble we wondered what we should find when we got there. All was well, but the next day we discovered that the close call we'd had was a landmine that fell in Neville Street. My husband's aunts lived in 58 Neville Street, and when he went there the house was totally destroyed. He was very distressed, as they had brought him up when his mother died when he was a child. He spent the day going round the hospitals and found them at last near home in St David's Hospital, shaken and bruised but otherwise unhurt.

A bomb damaged Allensbank Road during the last war.

A VE day street party at The Crescent, Fairwater, 1945.

They had been in the cupboard under the stairs and that was all that remained of the house. They had lost all their belongings and I can remember getting together clothes, shoes, handbags etc. to get them going again. Their names were Miss Lilian Morgan and Mrs Gertrude Smith, and after the war the house in Neville Street was rebuilt as flats and the aunts were very proud of their new home.

Sybil Josty

After the War

In May 1945, VE-Day arrived. The national rejoicing was overwhelming, although there was still a war in the Pacific. The population of Cardiff all seemed to converge on the area in front of the City Hall. We were there, and on that day there were impromptu dances and fun and games.

Bonfires were lit in many streets, giving the fire brigade some additional practice particularly where the fire was over a manhole cover and I can still visualize Mrs Henry, who was a large lady to say the least, dancing in the light of the bonfire flames. During the next few days there were street parties, and houses were decorated. Either by design or accident the various streets in Cathays did not hold their parties on the same day, and I managed to attend a few. There was still rationing of course, but the trestle tables down the middle of the streets were laden with food, drink and crackers, and there were races with prizes for everybody. To an eleven-year-old it was exciting and memorable. To grown ups it must have been a time when the world was happy – the fearful past had gone and the problems and worries of the future not even considered. Chris Jenkins, the hairdresser who lived in Rhigos Gardens, was a pioneer home cine enthusiast, and there may still be in existence amateur film of those exciting days and of the street parties.

Surprisingly VE-Day was soon followed by a General Election, the first in nine years. I took great interest in this, although not really understanding the issues, and recall attending a meeting at Cathays National School at which a young teacher called George Thomas spoke. George, as he was known to everybody, eventually became the Speaker of the House. Elections were then conducted in a quite different way. As there were no television, limited radio coverage and small newspapers, the candidates were forced to meet the voters face to face in the streets with the loudspeaker vans, and at well attended meetings. The result of the 1945 election, which Labour won by a landslide, was not announced for some days because of the need to transmit and count the services' votes from abroad.

Geoff Bray

King George VI Visit

When I was seventeen I started work in Currans Munitions, from December 1937 until January 1941. I was a lathe worker making shell cases. We worked three shifts: 6-2, 2-10 and 10-6. The night shift being the worst because of the air-raids of which there were many. There was no running to the shelters when the siren went. We had to stay working our machines until the red alert was sounded then down the shelter. It was very frightening and to keep our spirits up we used to sing to try and drown the noise of the guns and bombs. The factory had a few near misses from bombs. I used to cycle to work, from Henmen Street in Grangetown to the docks and back, which was about four miles each way. Often shrapnel was falling all around and I must say I was frightened. Penarth Road was open fields

King George VI watching June Williams at her machine.

in those days and there was nowhere to shelter if it got too bad so one had to cycle on regardless. One day, 9 February 1940, I even remember the date as it was special for me, King George VI came to visit which was very exciting as he stopped by my machine to watch me work and stayed sometime. I have a photograph of this; my little claim to fame. Unfortunately, the king did not speak to me. I was told beforehand, and probably the other girls as well: should the king stop at my machine I was to carry on with my work and not look up, which was a pity as he watched me work for about ten minutes. Why he chose to stop at my machine I will never know.

Mrs June Williams

Sylvia Kendrick, 1999.

Wartime Rations

I was fifteen when I went to work in the Direct Trading Company and then the war was on. It was rationing and I knew all the rations: two ounces of butter, a quarter of margarine, two ounces of tea, half-a pound of sugar. That was the weekly ration and a pot of jam once a month. Now and again they used to have something come in the shops like tins of salmon. They used to put names down and as the people had one of these tins their names would be crossed off the list and somebody else would have one.

Sylvia Kendrick

Underground Factory

During the war I started work in Currans and then I was transferred to Bath. I was there around twelve months or so, in the underground factory where they were made air plane engines which were later sent to Fulton in Bristol. My job was to check the condition of the air underground and I had a special pass which would allow me to go in any part of the factory. My boyfriend John Donovan made out he was eighteen and joined the Fleet Air Arm when he was only seventeen, after getting his mother to sign the papers. I contracted TB from working in the underground factory and was sent home. I was recovering in the Sanatorium Hospital on VJ Day when they let me out for the day to marry John who served in the navy for six years.

Emily Donovan

John Donovan who joined the Fleet Air Arm during the last war.

CHAPTER 6

Clothes and Fashion

Mackross was a popular department stores for many years.

My First Outfit

I remember my first outfit. I had a long grey coat and for fashion you had to have about four or five inches of dress showing beneath it. I had this royal blue dress showing beneath this long coat right down to my ankles. I wore a grey trilby with a feather: the bigger the better. You ought to have seen me. I thought it was marvellous.

Maud Jones

Permanent Waves

Hand-knitted garments were the usual wear for children in the winter with cotton dresses in the summer and navy serge shorts to the knees for boys. In June we could put away our winter clothes until mid-September as the season's weather was more predictable then.

The fashionable long singlets [hairstyle] for girls gradually gave way to the American Bob, the Shingle, the Clara Bow. Film star style and a fringe. When permanent waves were first introduced it was necessary to be wired-up to the machine in a most uncomfortable manner. Quite an ordeal, in fact. Young boys' heads were very closely cropped, short back and sides.

Ruth Hobbs

Open Drawers

I remember my mother used to wear open drawers. Just two legs and a band around with a button at the back. She also wore red flannel petticoats. They were quite fashionable.

Clarice Langdon

Ruby Howe, 1999.

Most Unfashionable Man

I'm the most unfashionable person of all time I should think. I kept myself clothed only to keep myself decent. I'm a little too old to change now.

John Attree

Make Do and Mend

I was never very fashion conscious myself. During the war we missed out. It was a question of make do and mend. I ironed one dress until it was nearly threadbare. But you had to make do.

Ruby Howe

John Attree, 1999.

Bowler hats were fashionable with these gentlemen in Kingsway in 1908.

Straw Hat and Gloves

If I had to go to town I wore a straw hat and gloves. There was no such thing as casual wear in those days. On a Sunday you dressed up not dressed down as they do today. Girls looked pretty and they wore more feminine things. Hairstyles were also neater and tidier.

Mrs John

Easter Bonnet

Fashions weren't so casual in those days. Everything had to match. A hat was very important especially at Easter time. When you went to town you had to be smartly dressed. Black was very fashionable before the last war. It was very stylish.

Ruth Hobbs

Siren Suits

I used to get a lot of army blankets and make stuff. I am pretty handy with my hands. I'd get a lot of stuff from people and turn them inside out and make things for children. I wouldn't charge the poor families. I'd do a lot of dressmaking, and we'd call them siren suits – they were all in one like jump suits – you were in and out of the shelters with the air raids and bombs.

Maud Jones

Evening Classes

I used to make my own clothes and my children's. I could knit and sew. I had no tuition, but I did go to evening classes when I got older.

Gladys Jenkins

Cresta Silks

I started work in Cresta Silks in High Street in the 1950s. I was paid £2 10s. We had many show business stars coming into the shop who were appearing at the New Theatre. I remember the singer Lita Rosa buying a gown which cost £400, a huge amount of money then. Needless to say, it was the most expensive gown shop in town. We stocked cashmere sweaters, silk scarves, wedding dresses and even jewellery.

Jacqueline Lee

Parachute Panels

I can remember parachute panels being sold coupon free during the war. They made good undies. Sometimes you could get a white flour sack with large black printing on it. We cut them up for tea towels. We didn't have a sewing machine so what we made we stitched by hand.

Reta Gale

Wives of channel pilots, c. 1898.

Minnie Stamp (née Taylor) sat for this portrait in 1930.

CHAPTER 7

Sport

Brian Lee with Brian Fletcher who will always be associated with Red Rum.

Point-To-Point

I was just sixteen years old when I took my father's advice and went on a bus ride to Rhiwbina Farm on the outskirts of Cardiff. The purpose of my visit was to attend, for the first time, a point-to-point meeting. It was held on 5 April 1952 and I still have the racecard. The Pentyrch Hunt Steeplechases proved something of a revelation to me and I soon became an ardent fan travelling by bus to other local point-to-points. I would follow my hero Bill Jones and favourite horses Sylvester 11, Cariff Princess, Spurn Head and Sally On. But little did I think then that, fourteen years later, I would be reporting on the sport for such esteemed publications as *The Sporting Life*, *Horse and Hound* and *Racing Post*. Or that I would write a book, *The Races Came Off: The Story of Point-To-Point Racing in South and West Wales*, about the history of the sport. Or that I would meet many of the

Pentyrch Hunt Point-To-Point racecard, 5 April 1952.

great names of the turf such as Sir Gordon Richards, Sir Harry Llewellyn, Lord John Oaksey, Johnny Francome, Peter Scudamore, Hywel Davies, Carl Llewellyn and Brian Fletcher who will always be associated with the legendary Red Rum. And to think it all really started that day my father persuaded me to go to the hunt races back in 1952.

Brian Lee

The Taff Swim

One of the annual events of Cardiff, when I was young was the Taff Swim. This was before the Cardiff Taff became the foul black sewer of later years. The swim, only a mile and a half or so, attracted male swimmers from all over the country. E.H. Temme, the channel swimmer from London, is one name I recall and Paolo Radmilovic and 'Leggy' Palmer were local swimmers who took part. It was no great feat of physical endurance. They all got in at Canton Bridge at the top of the tide, and were bourne downstream to be hauled out at Clarence Road Bridge. But they were heroes in the days before the mass media created champions overnight and every night. Because of the increasing pollution of the River Taff, the event was transferred to Roath Park Lake, but here it died because the water became infected with micro-organisms which stung the skin and

A path beside the River Taff, with swans swimming and on the bank.

Spectators at the Roath Park Lake Taff Swim, c. 1953.

Lord Mayor Alderman W.J. Hartland with Brian Lee outside City Hall, 1964.

did no end of damage to the eyes of small fish. I believe women swimmers competed in the Taff Swim for the first time in Roath Park Lake and the names of lady swimmers Valerie Davies and Freda Pawley come to mind. At that time, and especially for mixed swimming, men and women wore black cotton costumes, extra long from shoulder to thigh; the women's often with a short skirt. After immersion these costumes stretched and sagged and were unsightly garments. Thicker woollen costumes of various colours, which kept their shape and men's costumes began to be reduced to trunks in the 1930s.

Stanley J. Adams

In The Long Run

These days no one would give a second glance to the hundreds of joggers that can be seen plodding the streets of Cardiff. A far cry from the 1950s and 1960s when there were only a few of us long distance runners training for what was then the only real long distance event in Wales, the annual Welsh AAA Marathon. Unlike today's road running races, which attract thousands of competitors, this Welsh championship race rarely had more than a dozen or so starters. And life was more hazardous for us then. For the sight of a road runner in those days seemed to bring out the worst in people. Not content at shouting remarks like: 'Come on Chataway' or 'Here come Gordon Pirie' or 'Why don't you catch a bus?', they would swear at you. Motorists would take great delight in sounding their horns and frightening you as they sped past. Some were even mad enough to force you off the road. On one occasion a motorist wound down his window and spat at me! In 1964 I was selected to run from the City Hall to Mountain Ash with a message from the Lord Mayor, Alderman W.J. Hartland JP, which was to be read by Councillor Morgan before the start of the famous Nos Galan Road Races. A great honour, but I had only gone half-a-mile or so when I was almost knocked down by a bus in North Road! Road runners today are lucky in that they have dozens of marathons, half-marathons and shorter distances to choose from. These races are well organized and can be guaranteed to be run over the correct distances. Yet when I won the 1964 Glamorgan & Monmouthshire twenty miles championship beating Welsh international Ken Flowers in a time of 2 hours 2 minutes and 26 seconds the course was re-measured afterwards and found to be two miles too long! The previous year, when I had finished just 17 seconds behind Commonwealth Games marathon runner Ron Franklyn, the course proved to be nearly two miles too short! If there were feeding stations throughout these races then I cannot recall them. And proper road running shoes or trainers were the exception rather than the rule.

Even the 1948 Olympic silver medallist Welshman Tom Richards wore daps (plimsolls) when I ran against him in the 1957 Welsh Marathon which started and finished at Maindy Stadium. How I envy today's road runners.

Brian Lee

Welsh Powderhall Champion

My father, Charles Edmund Williams 'Eddie', who won the famous Welsh Powderhall Handicap Sprint at Taff Vale Park in Pontypridd in 1921, was born in Cathays on 18 June 1887. His father was William Richard Williams, a carpenter on the Taff Vale Railway. He was the third of six children – four boys and two girls. My father attended Albany Road Board School where he was prominent in sport. He was awarded the Mayor of Cardiff's prize at a sports meeting on 8 September 1900. He was a keen footballer from a young age, playing for Cathays Juniors and subsequently Cathays Association Football Club. In the season 1912/13 when my father was vice captain they won the first division of the Cardiff and District Football League and also the Lord Ninian Challenge and the Suggs Challenge Cups. He told me that he was offered terms to play professional football but declined on the grounds of insecurity. During the Great War he served in the Royal Artillery, initially in

France and then in Mesopotamia and rose to the rank of sergeant. He was a master carpenter by trade and later ran his own business as a builder. My dad obviously led a very active sporting life. He did not marry until he was forty-one – in November 1928 – and I was born in October 1929. We lived in Cwmdare Street in Cathays and he lived there until he died. During the latter part of his working life he worked for the Co-op.

My father was a rather shy man. He spent much time with his brothers, Arthur and Lloyd. They were members of the United Services Mess in Wharton Street. He died on the 13 November 1959, aged seventy-two, of cancer of the lung.

Len Williams

Eddie Williams winner of the world famous Welsh Powderhall Sprint.

The White Hope

There used to be, at the end of a corridor leading to the back of 4 St John's Square, a gymnasium – Peterson's Gymnasium and it was here trained the white hope of Wales in the boxing world, Jack Peterson, son of the owner, Pa Peterson. Although young Jack achieved the heavyweight championship of Britain, he laboured under two disabilities in a fiercely competitive calling. He lacked the economic drive to make good, and he was too nice a feller. He never had to fight to eat, like so many others who came up through the fairground boxing booths, and he lacked the killer instinct. When he was seventeen, I saw him, in his first professional fight, take on Leo Bandias, an Australian, in the Greyfriars Road Hall. Peterson won, although I didn't see the end because I had to dash off to catch a train for the night shift in Newport post office.

Stanley J. Adams

A Pig's Bladder

During the winter nights we would play rugby between the street lamps in Adam Street. The ball was a pig's bladder obtained from the slaughter house in Sanguar Street. The ball would often end up over the prison wall. I remember playing rugby in Sophia Gardens and we would all gather around the water fountain. My brothers Jack, Joey, Louise and me went North to play rugby league. Ringo, the youngest brother, stayed in Cardiff to play for Danny Davies's side in 1927.

Angelo Corsi

Shrugged Shoulders Help Beat All Blacks

Once upon a time forwards were seldom, if ever, expected to score tries in the Rugby

Sophia Gardens fountain where Angelo Corsi and friends would meet for rugby.

Union game. They were on the field to labour in the service of the more privileged: the stylish runners who created the memorable moments and the exciting events to thrill the watchers. This has all changed now and often forwards have taken matters into their own hands and done the bulk of the scoring. The donkeys share the limelight with the thoroughbreds. But, back in 1953 – the last time Wales defeated New Zealand, the back division was accepted as the strike force. They were the players who would decide the issue. Bleddyn Williams told his Cardiff forwards before they faced the All Blacks, 'Give me just two-fifths of the ball and we'll win the match. But without you we can't do it.' His forwards did their job and Cardiff won 8-3. Bleddyn Williams was captain again when Wales faced the tourists at the Arms Park a month later. Cliff Morgan, the outside half of unforgettable memory, remembered the tactics to be used: 'Bleddyn's plan was to tie in the New Zealand back row to prevent them mowing down our midfield. He said we were to throw long line outs. The signal for this was for scrum half Rex Willis to shrug his shoulders. What we didn't appreciate was the fact that Rex was always shrugging his shoulders. It was a habit of his! Little wonder just about every throw was long. A fluke, maybe – but it worked'. As with the heroic Cardiff forwards, who held out against an awesome assault when every moment we expected them to crumble, the Welsh pack also refused to buckle. 'How we came back to win I have never understood,' recalled Bleddyn. 'Where our forwards drew their strength and stamina to storm back in the last fifteen minutes will never be answered. It was a Welsh miracle of rugby football.' So it was a third successive defeat for the All Blacks at the Arms Park, this

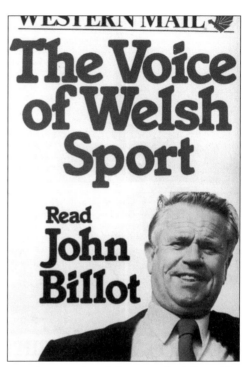

An advertising board showing John Billot – The Voice of Welsh Sport.

time 13-8, with an inspired cross-kick by Clem Thomas from near the touch line right across into midfield. There, Ken Jones swooped to collect the bounce and race clear to the posts in front of 56,000 spectators.

John Billot,
Former sports editor,
Western Mail

Table Tennis

We had a very strong Western Mail & Echo table tennis team. Fortunately we had some good table tennis tables in the work's canteen. One for practising on and one for

Western Mail & Echo table tennis team, c. 1936.

Western Mail & Echo soccer team, 1932.

playing matches. We played in the business league. We had three internationals in Fred O'Leary (for Ireland) and Charlie Radcliffe and Dewi Lewis (for Wales). And with these three playing then the rest of the team became very good and in 1936/37 we won the Cardiff & District league trophy. We had a lot of fun playing soccer as well. Though we were much better at table tennis.

Harry Ferris

Cardiff Dragons

In the early 1950s, I was a regular Cardiff Dragons speedway fan. The Penarth Road stadium was said to be one of the best speedway tracks in the country. I can remember in 1952 the Cardiff Dragons team beating Plymouth by 47 points to 37 points. The fans certainly had their money's worth that night with the track record being broken no fewer than five times. This was the year that the World Speedway Riders' Championship was held there. Teams from New Zealand, Sweden, and America took part. Kevin Hayden, 'Chum' Taylor and my own particular favourite rider Mick Holland are just three of the speedway stars that used to thrill the crowds every Thursday evening. As supporters of the Dragons team we would shout out 'Two, four, six, eight, who do we appreciate ... Cardiff Dragons!' The roar of the motorbikes, the smell of the fuel and the clouds of shale dust thrown up as the riders rounded a bend all made it very exciting to a young lad of fifteen or sixteen.

Brian Lee

Speedway riders in action, Penarth Road Stadium, 1951.

Acknowledgements

The following is a list of all those people, past and present, who contributed their memories and photographs for *Cardiff Voices* and without their help this book could never have been compiled. I beg forgiveness of any contributors who may have been inadvertently omitted from these acknowledgements.

Bill Barrett, Philip Donovan, Gladys Jenkins, Stanley J. Adams, Tegwen Hucklestone, Geoff Bray, Ruth Hobbs, Jos Dwyer, Owen Martin, Sylvia Kendrick, Marcia Williams, Mrs John, Audrey Anderson, Phyllis Anderson, Henry Britton, Joan Taylor, Gaynor Rosser, A. Glyn Davies, Jim Cowley, Len Williams, Stanley Sorenson, Alan T. Grainger, Maud Jones, Vince Jones, Allen Hambly, Mary Jackson, Margaret L. Jones, Ina Gale, Reta Gale, Ruby Howe, Marion Jenkins, John Attree, Ron Davies, Edward Kendrick, Donald Williams, Harry Ferris, Clarice Langdon, A. Knighton, Dennis Pope, Harry Welchman, Joan Burnell, Barbara Stone, Monica Walsh, Charles Harlin, Mrs J. Francis, Mary Jackson, Mrs R. Richards, Diana Prichard, Evelyn Pincott, Bill Brian, Margaret Williams, Betty McLeod, Thomas E. Broad, Sheilah Davies, Valerie Snell, Eirfryn Lowe, Sybil Josty, June Williams, Angelo Corsi, John Billot, Sheila Long, Jacqueline Lee. Meg Johnson, Emily Donovan, Barbara Hancock, Alun Sedgmore, Bill Penny, Aileen Lucas and Margaret Sidaway.

Special thanks to my project editor Jane Friel for giving me the opportunity to compile this book and for her help and encouragement. It has not always been possible to trace copyright on some of the photographs and I apologize for any inadvertent infringement.

Brian Lee

By the same author:

The Races That Came Off: the Story of Point-to-Point Facing in South and West Wales
The Great Welsh Sprint: the Story of the Welsh Powderhall Championship 1903-1934
Cardiff remembered
Cathays, Maindy, Gabalfa and Mynachdy
Central Cardiff
Central Cardiff: the second selection
Butetown and Cardiff Docks